Real Cheesy Facts About: Famous Authors

CRANE HILL
PUBLISHERS

Real Cheesy Facts About: Famous Authors

Copyright © 2006 by Crane Hill Publishers

ISBN-13: 978-1-57587-250-6
ISBN-10: 1-57587-250-1

Book design by Miles G. Parsons
Illustrations by Tim Rocks and Miles G. Parsons

Printed in the United States of America

Library of Congress Cataloging-in-Publication Data

Platt, Camille Smith.
  Real cheesy facts about-- famous authors / by Camille
Smith Platt.
      p. cm.
  ISBN-13: 978-1-57587-250-6
  1. Authors, American--Anecdotes 2. Authors, English--
Anecdotes 3. Authors--Anecdotes. 4. Authors, American--
Miscellanea. 5. Authors, English--Miscellanea. 6. Authors--
Miscellanea. I. Title.

  PS138.P55 2006
  820.9--dc22
    [B]

2006024772

Real Cheesy Facts About: Famous Authors

Camille Smith Platt

CRANE HILL
PUBLISHERS

TABLE OF CONTENTS

Chapter 1

Best-kept Secrets:
The Details They Never
Wanted You to Know

Best-kept Secrets: The Details They Never Wanted You to Know

Everyone has little secrets. You know, covert details about their lives that they would really rather remain unpublished. Unfortunately for these authors, their most hush-hush mysteries have now been let out of the bag. Here is the dirty laundry they hoped you would never find out.

THREE THINGS YOU NEVER KNEW ABOUT … F. SCOTT FITZGERALD

- He was named after Francis Scott Key, a distant relative famous for penning *The Star-Spangled Banner*.

- His wife, Zelda, developed schizophrenia and was permanently hospitalized in 1932. She died when a fire broke out at the Highland Mental Institution in Asheville, North Carolina, in 1948.

- An avid drinker, Fitzgerald died of a heart attack while visiting a friend. He was only forty-four years old.

★ ★ ★ ★ ★

My Lips Are Sealed: Maya Angelou

Her Big Secret: Before she hit the books, she hit the brothel.

The Juicy Details Unveiled: When literature lovers envision the beautiful imagery in the classic poem "I Know Why the Caged Bird Sings," thoughts of brothels and rowdy nightclubs hardly come to mind. But those who spent time with author Maya Angelou in her younger years know she sowed some wild oats in her day. A single mother struggling to support her young son, Angelou was once a San Diego madam. She also earned some extra cash by cooking at a Creole café, scraping paint off of old cars at a body shop, and running cable cars. It's hard to believe respected historic figures such as Dr. Martin Luther King Jr. could overlook such a shady past—he appointed Angelou as a coordinator of the Southern Christian Leadership Conference in the 1960s.

THREE THINGS YOU NEVER KNEW ABOUT ... MAYA ANGELOU

- She was born Marguerite Johnson.
- She was once kicked out of school for being afraid to speak in front of the class.
- She took a pilgrimage to Ghana in the 1960s so her son could attend the University of Ghanato and get in touch with his African roots.

★ ★ ★ ★ ★

My Lips Are Sealed: Bram Stoker

His Big Secret: The initial plans for his vampire were thrown in the trash.

The Juicy Details Unveiled: Bram Stoker's Count Dracula was originally supposed to be named Count Vampyre, but while researching the historic details for his book, he came across the new name, which meant "son of the dragon" or "son of the devil." It was the actual name of a fifteenth-century Romanian nobleman who became a hero when he fought off Turkish invaders. Dracula became tainted, however, by his reputation for brutally executing his prisoners. It was a perfect past for a monster, and Stoker had his protagonist.

LOVE'S LITTLE SURPRISES

Bram Stoker married one of author Oscar Wilde's ex-girlfriends in 1878.

★ ★ ★ ★ ★

MY LIPS ARE SEALED: THOMAS HARDY

His Big Secret: He hid the shady details of how hundreds of women cheated on their husbands.

The Juicy Details Unveiled: After Hardy published *Tess of the d'Urbervilles*, a controversial novel about a woman who becomes pregnant by a man who is believed to be her relative, he received scores of letters from women with similar dark pasts. The women poured out their private stories, revealing their guilt and asking Hardy what he thought they should do. Surprised that so many people would sign their names to such confidential, scandalous stories and send them to a stranger, Hardy didn't quite know what to do. A friend advised him not to reply (or call, as some women requested), so instead, he burned each letter. He was forever careful not to mention any of their names to his peers or interviewers for fear their identities would become publicly revealed.

★ ★ ★ ★ ★

My Lips Are Sealed: Charles Dickens

His Big Secret: He was nearly caught vacationing with his mistress.

The Juicy Details Unveiled:

Desperately trying to hide the fact that he was traveling with actress Ellen Ternan—who was rumored to have broken up his marriage—Charles Dickens told few people that he was involved in a serious train wreck. On June 9, 1865, six train cars plunged off a faulty bridge between London and Dover. Dickens was in the only first-class section that didn't jump the track. At first he rushed to aid the wounded, but when he realized the press would soon arrive and discover him with Ellen, he grabbed the manuscript he was working on (the novel *Our Mutual Friend*) and left the scene of the accident. Possibly due to the wreck, he struggled with swelling in his left foot for the rest of his life.

★ ★ ★ ★ ★

My Lips Are Sealed: F. Scott Fitzgerald

His Big Secret: His wife caught him plagiarizing.

The Juicy Details Unveiled:

The mastermind behind popular classics such as *The Great Gatsby*, F. Scott Fitzgerald was once accused of having trouble keeping his work original—his wife, Zelda, claimed he plagiarized things he found around the house. In a tongue-in-cheek review in the *New York Tribune* in 1922, she joked that on more than one occasion she recognized pieces of her husband's work as fragments from her old diaries and letters from friends. Call it secondhand inspiration, call it a temporary solution to writer's block—but some editors would call it theft.

★ ★ ★ ★ ★

My Lips Are Sealed: L. Frank Baum

His Big Secret: He sank like a brick.

The Juicy Details Unveiled: He may have been the creative inventor of Toto, the Tin Man, and those pesky singing munchkins, but author L. Frank Baum had quite a problem when it came to kicking back on a hot summer day. While his buddies were playing "beach bum" in the pool, he stayed on shore. Though Baum couldn't swim, he wasn't entirely afraid. To keep track of whether or not he was

L. Frank Baum wasn't the only writer who had a troubled relationship with water. *Lolita* author Vladimir Nabokov once said, "I dislike immersing myself in a swimming pool. It is, after all, only a big tub where other people join you — makes one think of those horrible Japanese communal baths, full of a floating family, or a shoal of businessmen."

getting into too-deep water, he would smoke a cigar while wading. If the water got high enough to put out his puffs, he would head for dry ground.

★ ★ ★ ★ ★

 MY LIPS ARE SEALED: JAMES THURBER

His Big Secret: He could barely see.

The Juicy Details Unveiled: Best known for his 1950s short stories and sketches published in *The New Yorker*, James Thurber was nearly blind. He lost one eye in an accident with a bow and arrow at just six years old. Because the first eye wasn't removed immediately, the second became infected and grew weaker as he got older. Over time, the disability required Thurber to write and draw on large sheets of white paper with chunky black crayons, or on black paper with thick sticks of white chalk. Neuroscientists later proposed that he had Charles Bonnet syndrome, which causes people with visual impairments to hallucinate. It's no wonder his handwriting and sketches seemed so eerie.

★ ★ ★ ★ ★

My Lips Are Sealed: E.E. Cummings

His Big Secret: He hated it when people wrote his name using all lowercase letters.

The Juicy Details Unveiled: Born Edward Estlin Cummings, poet and playwright E.E. Cummings was duped when his publishers went behind his back and started publishing his name in a modern-looking lowercase form: e. e. cummings. Despite stories that circulated during the nineteenth century, Cummings never legally changed his name to the lowercase version—in fact, he hated it. While famous for his unorthodox use of punctuation and capitalization in his poetry, he said it belonged nowhere in his byline, and he never endorsed the change.

> **THE SPY WHO TAGGED ME**
> While serving in an ambulance unit during the First World War, E.E. Cummings and friend William Slater Brown were arrested under suspicion of espionage. They may have been pacifists, but they were not spies. After a few weeks in a Normandy detention center, Cummings was released and later drafted into the army.

★ ★ ★ ★ ★

My Lips Are Sealed: Edgar Allan Poe

His Big Secret: He's not buried where you think he is.

The Juicy Details Unveiled: Relatives of renowned poet Edgar Allan Poe aren't quite sure if the body buried at Poe's gravesite is actually his. Poe was originally buried in 1849 amid other lesser-known people at Baltimore's Westminister Hall and Burying Ground, which has since been annexed by the University of Maryland School of Law. In 1875, a group of ambitious schoolchildren raised the cash to erect a memorial and move Poe's remains to a more prestigious spot near the front gate. However, no one thought to tell the crew in charge of digging up Poe's body that all of the headstones had been rotated to the west in 1864—

positioning the bodies behind the stones instead of in front. They most likely dug in the wrong spot, and today many speculate the reburied remains are actually of a teenager from the Maryland Militia named Private Philip Mosher Jr.

THE MYSTERY OF THE POE TOASTER

Every January 19 since 1949, an unnamed man with a black hood and a silver-tipped cane has visited Edgar Allan Poe's grave. He toasts the deceased author with a glass of Martel cognac, then departs while it is still dark, leaving behind the half-full liquor bottle and three red roses—one for Poe, one for Poe's mother, and one for Poe's wife.

★ ★ ★ ★ ★

MY LIPS ARE SEALED: FYODOR DOSTOEVSKY

His Big Secret: He made lofty wagers.

The Juicy Details Unveiled: *Crime and Punishment* may be remembered as one of Dostoevsky's most ingenious works, but few know that he wrote the book in a hurry—he was in desperate need of a gambling fix. Having lost thousands of dollars to his gambling addiction, Dostoevsky was penniless (and longing for another trip to the casino). Ironically, he was so poor that he wrote *The Gambler* at the same time, rushing to finish it for another publisher who threatened to take over all of Dostoevsky's copyrights if he did not settle his debts.

READ, AIM, SNICKER

In 1849, Russian writer Fyodor Dostoevsky was sentenced to death for anti-government revolts against Tsar Nikolai I. However, his captors mocked the execution and left him standing blindfolded in the snow, anticipating the sting of bullets from a firing squad. After their cruel joke came to a close, they instead sentenced him to manual labor.

OTHER AUTHORS WITH GAMBLING DEBTS

- Leo Tolstoy
- Edgar Allan Poe

18

★ ★ ★ ★ ★

My Lips Are Sealed: Stephen King

His Big Secret: He's more like his characters than you think he is.

The Juicy Details Unveiled: King is known around the world for his suspenseful, chilling reads, but few fans know that his own life once reflected the unstable antagonists of his novels. For years King refused to admit his transgressions, that is, until his buddies stole one of his trashcans and dumped it on the floor in front of him. A soiled confession of King's secrets—the pile of beer cans, Valium, NyQuil, and Xanax—forced him to come clean about his addictions. It was then that he finally admitted the crazed father

DID YOU KNOW

Although he believed the conflict was unconstitutional, Stephen King was nearly drafted into the Vietnam War, but a doctor determined he had high blood pressure, flat feet, poor vision, and a punctured eardrum.

he wrote about in *The Shining* was not based on his own father, as he had once claimed, but on himself. He cleaned up his act and was sober by the late 1980s.

★ ★ ★ ★ ★

My Lips Are Sealed: Lewis Page Mercier

His Big Secret: He screwed up several historic Jules Verne books.

The Juicy Details Unveiled: Although English-speaking countries have long criticized Frenchman Jules Verne's writing, his misunderstood literature can only be blamed on the Brits. One man in particular, a book translator named Lewis Page Mercier, allegedly took it upon himself to change the author's manuscripts without permission from the publisher. Feeling that some of Verne's content was a bit too critical of the British Empire, Mercier cut out the details of Captain Nemo's political ties in the 1870 sci-fi novel *Twenty Thousand Leagues Under the Sea.* He also hated the metric system and made a mess of Verne's numbers in an attempt to convert them to something more understandable—sometimes he converted the figures to Imperial,

sometimes he kept them in metric but changed the units to Imperial, and sometimes he accidentally dropped the numbers altogether. The laziness made Verne look like a babbling fool in great need of a calculator (if not a math tutor). In 1965, some of his works were re-translated in their original form, but many copies full of errors still exist.

Jules Verne's publishers often told him his anti-Semitism and pessimistic views of human progress were too dark for his readers. Publisher Pierre-Jules Hetzel changed the endings of several of Verne's books to lighten the mood:

- *Mysterious Island* (1874)—A tale of Americans stranded in the South Pacific, Verne's original ending described survivors as living the rest of their lives nostalgically, missing the island. Hetzel rewrote them as heroes who build a replica of the island so they can live happily ever after.

- *Twenty Thousand Leagues Under the Sea* (1870)—In Verne's first draft, the valiant Captain Nemo was introduced as a Polish noble, bitter that his family had been murdered under Russian oppression from 1863–1864. Hetzel feared Russia would ban the book and upset its ally, France, and instead described Nemo as a Hindu who resents the British for their conquest of India.

★ ★ ★ ★ ★

MY LIPS ARE SEALED: HENRY DAVID THOREAU

His Big Secret: He never got a diploma because he was too cheap.

The Juicy Details Unveiled: Thoreau graduated from Harvard University in 1837, but because of his own frugalness (and stubbornness), he never received an official diploma. Legend holds that the college required a $5 payment before graduation, but Thoreau refused to shell out that kind of money for a "piece of paper." Unfortunately, the college rules stated that the Master of Arts degree held no academic merit unless the fee was paid in full.

My Lips Are Sealed: JD. Salinger

His Big Secret: He freaked out when his publisher put his face on his book.

The Juicy Details Unveiled: Salinger was not happy with the first edition of *The Catcher in the Rye* because it had a big picture of his face on the dust jacket. Although he reveled in the success of big sales, he was annoyed by everyone who began to recognize him.

After flunking out of one private high school as a young man, author J.D. Salinger studied at Valley Forge Military Academy in Pennsylvania. One year he got an 88 in English, 88 in French, 76 in German, 79 in History, and 88 in Dramatics. His IQ was tested as 115, and he was a member of the glee club, aviation club, and French club, as well as the literary editor of the yearbook. He began writing short stories by flashlight under the covers after "lights out" and dreamed of one day selling them to Hollywood.

Salinger quickly got tired of dodging autograph and advice-seeking fans. He called the attention "demoralizing." As a result, very little is known about his personal life, particularly his childhood and teenage years. He says he won't talk about "that David Copperfield kind of crap." Years ago, he wouldn't even tell interviewers what contemporary writers he preferred. He always seemed nervous about publicity.

My Lips Are Sealed: Shel Silverstein

His Big Secret: He was a pal of Playboy bunnies.

The Juicy Details Unveiled: Famed for the ever-popular *The Giving Tree* and *Where the Sidewalk Ends*, children's author Shel Silverstein, who died in 1999, wasn't the innocent rhyming writer most parents thought he was. In fact, he began his career as a photographer, writer, and cartoonist for *Playboy* magazine. He ended up living in the Playboy Mansion and continued to write occasional pieces for the raunchy publication up until a year before his death. When he wasn't babbling with blondes, Silverstein was also dreaming up songs—he wrote the lyrics for "A Boy Named Sue" for Johnny Cash and "One's On the Way" for Loretta Lynn.

★ ★ ★ ★ ★

My Lips Are Sealed: Kingsley Amis

His Big Secret: He was bored while "fighting" for his country.

The Juicy Details Unveiled: *Lucky Jim* (1954) author Kingsley Amis is a veteran of the Second World War, but don't let the heroic label fool you—he spent his entire

tour in a car. After training for months doing cross-country runs, shooting muskets, and making smoke bombs, Amis never used his skills once. His unit spent its time "at war" driving across Europe, nowhere near the front lines. He never fired a shot, and he never marched a step.

DID YOU KNOW

When Kingsley Amis first joined the army, another recruit told him his name was too hard to pronounce. Amis told him his middle name was actually William, but the recruit didn't like that either. Instead everyone called him Bill.

★ ★ ★ ★ ★

My Lips Are Sealed: Alexandre Dumas

His Big Secret: He didn't write most of his own books.

The Juicy Details Unveiled:
Although he publicly receives full credit for the creepy *The Count of Monte Cristo*, writer Alexandre Dumas actually did not pen much of the manuscript himself. To save time, he liked to use ghostwriters such as the famed Auguste Maquet, a history teacher who originally wrote the outline for *Monte Cristo* and much of *The Three Musketeers*. Dumas would take the rough draft from him and fill in the holes with quotes, details, and the last few chapters. All told, Dumas used seventy-three assistants to publish 250 books.

FROM RICHES TO RAGS
Although his writing earned him riches—he once brought in more than 200,000 francs per year—Alexandre Dumas spent much of his life in debt, due to his lavish lifestyle.

★ ★ ★ ★ ★

THEIR LIPS ARE SEALED: ROBERT AND ELIZABETH BARRETT BROWNING

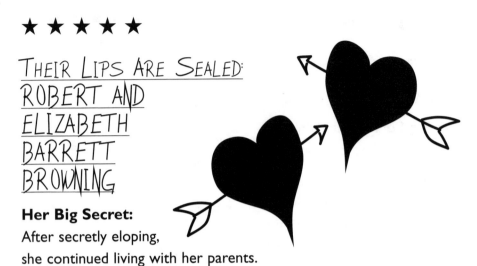

Her Big Secret:
After secretly eloping,
she continued living with her parents.

The Juicy Details Unveiled: Because she suffered injuries from a riding accident and the grief of her young brother's drowning, Elizabeth Barrett had spent most of her life locked up in her room, devoid of social interaction.

She would spend entire days doing nothing but reading books and plays on her father's sofa. When Robert first wrote her a letter to say that he admired one of her pieces of writing, she did what any woman would do—she sat around and waited for more love letters. The two became pen pals (she often edited his work) and finally met in May of 1845. Although

LOVE'S LITTLE SURPRISES

The Brownings weren't the only poets to try and hide a secret marriage. In 1601, John Donne married Ann More, the niece of his boss, Sir Thomas Egerton. Egerton was so angry that he had him fired and put in jail for the lie. He even tried to have their marriage annulled.

she rarely even got up off the
sofa to greet him when he
visited her, the two were
married the following year.
Afraid to tell her parents of her

> The first book a young
> Robert Browning ever
> purchased was *Oassian*.

marriage, she continued to live at home and took off her wedding
ring so they wouldn't know of her secret marriage.

★ ★ ★ ★ ★

My Lips Are Sealed: Dr. Seuss

His Big Secret: He was a grinch.

The Juicy Details Unveiled: Although remembered as a lyrical,
fun-rhyming poet who entertained children of all ages with his tales
of Whoville and green eggs and ham, Seuss actually has been accused
of writing about his own bad attitudes in *The Grinch Who Stole
Christmas*. The author's license plate read GRINCH, and in the book
the Grinch complains of putting up with the Whos' Christmas cheer
for the past 53 years—which was Seuss's age when he wrote the
book. Seuss was never fond of noise and public celebrations. In fact,

TALES OF THE RUDE AND CRUDE

During World War I, Theodore Seuss Geisel (or as most know
him, Dr. Seuss) was not ashamed of his German heritage.
However, the other kids in school nicknamed him The Kaiser and
threw rocks at him as he walked home from school. This
ostracizing may be why he avoided crowds for most of his life.

he reportedly complained about having to answer the door on his birthday when children would come by to sing to him. He would have preferred to be in Las Vegas alone.

★ ★ ★ ★ ★

MY LIPS ARE SEALED: DAVID MCCULLOUGH

His Big Secret: He thought he had one, but the beans were spilled years ago.

The Juicy Details Unveiled: After years of secrecy, *1776* author David McCullough has admitted to the public that while in college, he was a member of Yale University's elite Skull and Bones secret society. However, for years he was unaware that the club published membership lists up until 1971. McCullough isn't alone—other famous faces from the Skull and Bones listing include Presidents Howard Taft and George W. Bush, FedEx founder Frederick Smith, *New York Times* general manager Amory Howe Bradford, and a number of U.S. Senators.

★ ★ ★ ★ ★

My Lips Are Sealed: William Blake

His Big Secret: He was a part of the Gordon Riots.

The Juicy Details Unveiled:
While studying at London's Royal Academy in 1780, William Blake was a professional engraver eager to rebel against anything politically correct. In fact, in July he gathered together his favorite troublemaking pals and ran the unruly mob through Newgate Prison. They kept blue ribbons in their caps to symbolize their support of the American colonies. In response, King George III set up the city's first police force to help prevent such riots from happening again.

LOVE'S LITTLE SURPRISES

Both a poet and a professional engraver, William Blake married a poverty-stricken young girl named Catherine Boucher in 1782. She was so illiterate that she could only sign their wedding contract with an X.

★ ★ ★ ★ ★

My Lips are Sealed: IAN FLEMING

His Big Secret: He kept a diary.

The Juicy Details Unveiled: *James Bond* writer Ian Fleming kept a "book of golden words," a diary with phrases, character names, and quotes he wanted to save for future book ideas. For example, he kept note of a Bulgar proverb that read, "My enemy's enemy is my friend" and good villain names such as Mr. Szasz. He got the name James Bond from a book called *Birds of the West Indies*, written by an ornithologist named James Bond. After Fleming's famous books were published, Bond's wife wrote him a letter to thank him for using her husband's name.

★ ★ ★ ★ ★

My Lips are Sealed: WILKIE COLLINS

His Big Secret: He took opium to relieve pain ... then he took it again ... and again.

The Juicy Details Unveiled: A longtime pal of Charles Dickens, this old author had a heck of a case of arthritis, then known as "rheumatic gout." His joints needed some serious relief, but Collins popped his pain pills way too often. As a result, he became delusional, paranoid, and in the company of an invisible friend named Ghost Wilkie. Whether this new pal was an original or simply a version of his pesky alter ego, we may never know. Collins was so high on opium while he was writing the novel *The Moonstone* that when he finished, he had no recollection of coming up with large chunks of the book.

Chapter 2

A Few of Their
Favorite Things

A Few of Their Favorite Things

If you ran into J.K. Rowling or Woody Allen tomorrow, how would you steal another minute of their time? Sure, you could wave and hold out something for them to sign like all the other annoying fans—or you could use some inside information to tap into what makes them tick when they're off the clock. Run into Stephen King? Grab a catcher's mitt. Isaac Asimov? Maybe a Dr. Spock figurine. Here's the skinny on your favorite authors—what they value, where they chill, and whom they adore.

Mark Twain loved the grace and independence of cats. He named his pet kittens Sin, Sourmash, Satan, Blatherskite, and Beelzebub. In *Puddn'head Wilson*, he wrote, "A house without a cat—a well-fed, petted and properly revered cat—may be a home, but how can it prove its title?"

★ ★ ★ ★ ★

CHEAP CIGARS

Mark Twain once estimated that he went through three hundred cheap, strong cigars every month. His peers actually believed that was an understatement. If he was on vacation and needed to get some work done, he would allow himself

fifteen cigars every five hours. As he smoked, he would play billiards for hours on end. His billiard room was a true man's sanctuary, decorated with pool cues, wine bottles, and pipes. When he first married, he promised his wife that he would cut back and light up only once a week. The resolution didn't last long. The combination of writer's block and publisher deadlines drove him back to his old habits. Ignorant of the damage he was doing to his lungs, Twain thought it was a harmless pastime.

THE LAZY DAYS OF SUMMER ... AND FALL ... AND WINTER
In 1907, Mark Twain said that for several decades he had spent only three months writing each year. He spent the rest of his time on vacation.

★ ★ ★ ★ ★

A PLASTER DINOSAUR FOOTPRINT

In his home in La Jolla, California, **Dr. Seuss kept a rather unusual memento** on display for years—a plaster cast of a huge dinosaur track

> ## LOVE'S LITTLE SURPRISES (OR LACK THEREOF)
> Dr. Seuss and his wife, Helen, never had children. When asked about his empty nest, he often replied, "You have 'em, I'll amuse 'em."

once found in his hometown, Springville, Massachusetts. It didn't add much to the décor of the home, but the footprint was a gift from his father. It reminded him that even after death, anyone could leave a mark on the world, something he strove to do for the rest of his life.

★ ★ ★ ★ ★

THE CLARINET

The king of all things creative and quirky, **writer Woody Allen has played the clarinet since he was a teenager**. Born Allen Stewart

Königsberg, he even came up with his own stage name at age sixteen as a tribute to famous clarinetist Woody Herman. Allen has performed multiple times since the 1960s. He even tooted his woodwind with the Preservation Hall Jazz Band on the Sleepers soundtrack. His band, Woody Allen and His New Orleans Jazz Band, plays every Monday at The Carlyle Hotel in Manhattan.

SPORTS INJURIES

Although injuries often serve as devastating, career-ending moments for athletes, **a track-and-field injury prompted author Nicholas Sparks to write.** He first picked up a pen while benched from the University of Notre Dame track team, and he hasn't put it down since.

DID YOU KNOW?

Woody Allen was only nineteen years old when he started writing for *The Ed Sullivan Show* and *The Tonight Show*.

BASEBALL

Stephen King loves the Boston Red Sox and often includes the team in his writing. One of his books, *The Girl Who Loved Tom Gordon* (1999),

An avid baseball fan, Stephen King coached his son's team to the Little League championship game in 1989.

features the team's famous pitcher as the main character. He also co-wrote *Faithful: Two Diehard Boston Red Sox Fans Chronicle the Historic 2004 Season* after the team won the 2004 American League Championship Series and World Series. King frequently attends both home and away games.

★ ★ ★ ★ ★

TALL POLITICIANS

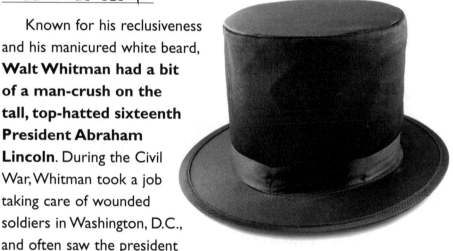

Known for his reclusiveness and his manicured white beard, **Walt Whitman had a bit of a man-crush on the tall, top-hatted sixteenth President Abraham Lincoln.** During the Civil War, Whitman took a job taking care of wounded soldiers in Washington, D.C., and often saw the president around the city. One of his most famous poems, "O Captain! My Captain!"—made famous by the film Dead Poets Society—was Whitman's way of expressing his grief after Lincoln's assassination in 1865.

★ ★ ★ ★ ★

COMMUNISM (SORT OF)

Born to a white shoe keeper and a black schoolteacher in the early 1900s, **poet Langston Hughes had a thing for the Commies.** The battle between segregation and civil rights was at its peak in the South, and the party's promises of fair fortunes tickled his ears. Hughes already had an in with the CPUSA—they often published his poems in their newspaper. His interest turned out to be more of an infatuation than a full-fledged political affair, however. While Hughes was occasionally involved in Communist-led groups, he quickly backed off when the House of Representative's investigating committee paid him a visit in 1953. He never officially joined the Communist party, and he passionately denied ever being a Communist at heart.

★ ★ ★ ★ ★

GREEN THUMBS

U.S. poet Thedore Roethke may have won the Pulitzer Prize for his book *The Waking* in 1954, but putting pen to paper wasn't always his most passionate hobby. For much of his life, Roethke had a thing for gardening. His father had owned a greenhouse, and during his childhood Roethke spent endless hours poking around the garden. The skills stuck with him as much of his poetry reflected on nature.

Theodore Roethke died of a heart attack while swimming in a pool in 1963. The pool was later filled in and today stands as a moss garden on Bainbridge Island, Washington—but there is no sign labeling it as the writer's place of passing.

Scotland's Sir Walter Scott also had a thing for working the land. His friends sent him acorns by the cartful, enough to plant his own forest, some said. He became so busy digging and leveling out his land for the plants that he had to hire a tutor to care for his son during the day.

TALES OF THE RUDE AND CRUDE

Although Sir Walter Scott's son's tutor, George Thomson, had an amputated leg, he had to walk to the Scott home every day until he was eventually invited to move in.

★ ★ ★ ★ ★

SLAPSTICK COMEDY

Best known for his poem "The Love Song of J. Alfred Prufrock," which he wrote at just twenty-two years old, American-born poet T.S. Eliot had one true love late in life— Groucho Marx. Eliot exchanged friendly letters with the comedian and even hung Marx's portrait in his home next to the likes of writers William Yeats and Paul Valery.

MODERN REFERENCES TO MR. PRUFROCK

Written from the perspective of an old man who regretted never taking a risk for love, T.S. Eliot's "The Love Song of J. Alfred Prufrock" has been hailed as an icon in American pop culture:

- Simon and Garfunkel's song "The Dangling Conversation" (made famous by Joan Baez) was written as a parallel to the poem.

- Musicians the Crash Test Dummies released a single called "Afternoons and Coffee Spoons" in the 1990s that mentioned the poem.

- In the film *Apocalypse Now*, Dennis Hopper plays a photojournalist who quotes the poem.

★ ★ ★ ★ ★

CUTE QUAIL

John Steinbeck, author of *Of Mice and Men* and *The Grapes of Wrath*, **took to boating and fishing on San Francisco Bay**, which helped trim down the grocery bill on his $25-a-month budget. He had always wanted to hunt quail for dinner but told a reporter from the *New York World Telegraph* in 1937 that "every time I see one around the house I dash in and get a gun, and get it to my shoulder, and then I can't shoot." The birds just looked so cute that he couldn't pull the trigger. Embarrassed that he had just told such a silly story about himself, Steinbeck admitted to the reporter that it was the first time he had ever been interviewed—"and be damned sure that it's the last," he said. It wasn't.

DID YOU KNOW

Steinbeck was terrible with punctuation, but his wife proofread all of his writing and caught the errors before they went to his editor.

When Steinbeck had friends over to his California home, he would keep the beer cold by putting it on the bottom of his swimming pool.

★ ★ ★ ★ ★

SCI-FI STUFF

Long before the cult-classic jargon of *Star Trek*, one of history's greatest writers had a secret guilty pleasure—he was a sci-fi junkie. The penman of the famed *Foundation Trilogy,* Isaac Asimov loved science-fiction magazines. The obsession began in his early teenage years when he reveled in the excitement of his favorite heroes—Shadow and Doc Savage—and dreamed about outer space, time travel, and the mysterious unknown. He wrote letters to the editors of his favorite magazines, trying to get his own sci-fi short stories printed. Asimov even offered the magazines advice, asking the staff to smooth out the rough edges of the paper they printed on and

> Isaac Asimov's fascination with science fiction as a boy led him to write his first story, *Cosmic Corkscrew*, at just seventeen years old.

giving them his opinion on his favorite stories. Although he rarely received a response, Asimov did become pen pals with the other science-fiction junkies who had their letters published in the magazines. They frequently exchanged issues and stories through the mail.

★ ★ ★ ★ ★

PARTIAL BIOGRAPHERS

Robert Frost couldn't have been more upset with his choice of a biographer. Lawrance Thompson, a curator of rare books at the Princeton University Library, was an acclaimed writer who spent thirty-five years working on the book. Frost was furious with his honesty. The men's relationship was often strained, as Frost believed Thompson wrote too much about the negative side of his character, describing him as psychotic, jealous, resentful, and vindictive. However, ultimately Frost believed Thompson had simply tired of the project and was describing his own attitude.

LAWSUITS

Most authors wouldn't be pleased to find out that their highly anticipated work was prematurely put on the shelves, but *Harry Potter* mogul **J.K. Rowling made millions on the mishap.** On June 19, 2003, Rowling found out that the *New York Daily News* had picked up a copy of *Harry Potter and the Order of the Phoenix* at a local health store and printed information about the plotline before its true release-date two days later. The article also included a photo of an inside spread of the book, with two pages perfectly readable. Her fans may have had the secrets spoiled, but Rowling raked in $100 million.

> J.K. Rowling is a fan of actor Aaron Sorkin from the American television show *The West Wing.*

HANGING OUT WITH HENRY

Ralph Waldo Emerson and Henry David Thoreau were great pals. The land where Thoreau built his cabin on Walden Pond belonged to Emerson, and Emerson hired Thoreau to perform odd jobs at his house for extra money. In fact, after leaving Walden, Thoreau lived in Emerson's house while he was

away on tour. However, the friendship soured after Emerson gave his buddy some bad business advice (he told him to publish his first book without many edits and advised him to use a publisher who made him take responsibility for much of the losses). The book bombed, and Thoreau was in debt.

★ ★ ★ ★ ★

MAGIC

Convinced that his hero Harry Houdini was possessed by supernatural powers, author Arthur Conan Doyle was amazed. The two men were friends for a time—until Houdini tried to convince him that the tricks were simply magic. Bitterly disagreeing on the issue of just how "real" the tricks were, the two butted heads until they had a very public falling out.

★ ★ ★ ★ ★

DEATH ROW INMATES

While working on his final research for the novel *In Cold Blood*, **Truman Capote desperately needed access to real, hardened criminals** at the state penitentiary in

DID YOU KNOW

While researching for *In Cold Blood*, Truman Capote became pen pals with two convicted criminals on death row who requested two things from him—a dictionary and a thesaurus. They wanted their descriptions of prison life to be accurate and sound smart, but their verbage was superfluous. One wrote that he had "many diverse subjects I am desirous to discuss."

Kansas. He found his men on death row, living with nothing more than a cot and a toilet. They showered once a week. However, to convince authorities to let him have at-will contact and mail privileges with two criminals (he was neither a relative or a lawyer) he bribed prison authorities with $10,000. The inmates, Perry and Dick, wrote him letters by the hundreds describing life behind bars—and the book was a hit.

★ ★ ★ ★ ★

Making Opinions Known

Novelist Iain Banks loves to heckle the editors of *New Scientist* magazine for their notes on creationism. If that weren't enough, he is also a member of a left-wing British political group that has campaigned to have Prime Minister Tony Blair impeached for his support of the invasion of Iraq. To protest the Brits having joined the war, Banks publicly ripped up his passport and threw it down on Downing Street.

> While a college student at Stirling University, Banks was an extra in the filming of the final scene of Monty Python and the Holy Grail at Doune Castle in Scotland.

★ ★ ★ ★ ★

New Husbands

Romance novelist Danielle Steel has always been known for her ability to describe lovers in bliss... but, unfortunately, she was rarely putting her own love life on paper. In fact, Steel has been married a total of five times. Her first wedding, at age eighteen, was to Claude-Eric Lazard. The couple had one daughter before she moved onto her second beau—a convicted rapist named Danny Zugelder. It wasn't long before they separated and Steel found herself pregnant—out of wedlock—by a druggie named William Toth. To give their son a daddy (for a short while), the couple got married. Her fourth husband, John Traina, had two sons of his own. The couple also had four daughters and a son... but, as usual, Steel moved on when Tom Perkins came around.

SHOTS OF CAFFEINE

Honore de Balzac was a maniac when it came to his work. He would stay up writing for fifteen hours at a time, throwing back as many cups of black coffee as he could. It's a wonder he kept up the social life he needed in order to complete the research for his books. In fact, many of his stories were based on conversations he overheard at parties. As he sucked down the caffeine, Balzac would edit his work over and over, annoying his printers with obscure last-minute changes.

★ ★ ★ ★ ★

DONATING TO CHARITY

MGM Studios often turns to secondhand clothes at garage sales around Hollywood, so while preparing for the 1939 film *The Wizard of Oz*, based on the book by L. Frank Baum, they hit the sales for some costumes. Ironically, when *Wizard* actor Frank Morgan put on his wardrobe for filming one day, he noticed a label on his overcoat. It read "Property of L. Frank Baum." Morgan got a laugh out of it, but after filming, Baum's wife looked at the costume and confirmed that it had been the author's. They had donated the jacket to charity several months before.

Chapter 3

Worst Week Ever:
The Bizarre (& Sometimes
Scary) Lives of
Thriller Writers

Worst Week Ever: The Bizarre (& Sometimes Scary) Lives of Thriller Writers

There are a number of circumstances that qualify a person officially having a horrible day. Some people have writer's block while all of their buddies come up with terrifying original tales. Some are smashed to pieces by an out-of-control driver while taking a Sunday stroll. Others wind up in jail, in an embarrassing costume, or in a shark's mouth. These authors take the cake in terms of the wacky predicaments in which they so often found themselves.

Agatha Christie learned much of what she knew about poison and pain while working as a pharmacist during World War I. She did not begin writing until her sister, who had always loved mysteries, challenged her to write a detective story.

53

★ ★ ★ ★ ★

AND THEN THERE WAS ONE

Whodunit writer Agatha Christie and her husband, Archie, once lived a rather posh life of travel and golf—that is, until he told her he was in love with another woman. When Christie freaked out and disappeared for ten days, the country panicked. Press, police, and detectives combed the neighborhood and eventually found her in a small-town hotel staying under an unusual pseudonym—the name of her husband's mistress. Now, decades later, only her daughter knows what she did during those mysterious ten days.

★ ★ ★ ★ ★

KING'S BIG BREAK

In the late 1990s, Stephen King was taking a stroll before joining his family for a screening of *The General's Daughter* when a van suddenly sped over a hill and threw him fourteen feet into the air. Medics airlifted him to a nearby hospital, but his lung collapsed—and doctors realized his leg was shattered, his hip and ribs were broken, and his spine was chipped in eight different places. After weeks in the hospital and even longer in physical therapy, King finally sat down to finish *On Writing*, but he was in such terrible pain after only thirty minutes of sitting down that he was forced to take lengthy breaks. One good thing did come out of his extensive time in the hospital—the experience inspired him to write the pilot episode of ABC's *Kingdom Hospital.*

PAYBACK'S A CINCH

Shortly after his recovery, Stephen King plotted revenge on the vehicle that crushed him in 1999—he bought it for $1,500 and then had it destroyed to prevent it from ever showing up on eBay.

THREE THINGS YOU NEVER KNEW ABOUT ... STEPHEN KING

- His mom worked in the kitchen of a mental institution when he was a child.
- Although he usually types on an Apple computer, he wrote the first draft of *Dreamcatcher* with a notepad and a fountain pen.
- He reads for four hours a day and writes for four hours a day. It is the only way to become a good writer, he says.

★ ★ ★ ★ ★

NIGHTMARE ON NAME STREET

Famous for works such as *The Mummy*, *The Witching Hour*, and *Interview with the Vampire,* **Anne Rice had no scarier day than the day her birth certificate was formally engraved**—with the name Howard Allen. Her parents wanted desperately to preserve their legacy in their daughter by incorporating both of their names—Katherine Allen and Howard O'Brien—in hers. However, Rice was mortified and tried out a series of new pseudonyms at school until she finally settled on Anne.

★ ★ ★ ★ ★

SUPER FANS GO OVERBOARD

Infatuation may be one form of flattery, but when it comes to obsessed readers, this tale of super-literate enthusiasts takes the cake. Giddy about their chance to see their names in print, nineteen lucky readers paid to become part of a permanent piece of literary history. The bidding was a fundraiser for the First Amendment Project, a nonprofit group that protects freedom of information and self-expression. Participants pulled out their checkbooks in hopes of being named as a person or place in upcoming works by authors Stephen

DID YOU KNOW

Much of author Anne Rice's fictional writing reflects her real life struggles. For example:

When the vampire Louis grieves the loss of young Claudia in *Interview with the Vampire*, Rice is really conveying her own sorrow over the death of her own daughter, Michele.

When Tonio struggles with an alcoholic mother in *Cry to Heaven*, it reflects the problems Rice had with her own mother.

King, John Grisham, and Lemony Snicket. Super fan Pam Anderson of Fort Lauderdale, Florida, shelled out a whopping $25,100 so her brother, Ray Huizenga, could find his name in Stephen King's *Cell*. However, the "honor" was not guaranteed to be flattering—the novel is about a trouble-making mob of zombies. Only John Grisham promised his winning bidder would be cast as a "good guy."

SUPER FAN AUCTION

- David Brin—Winner can choose for their name to represent either a moon about to collide with a planet, a mystifying new disease, or a species of aliens. **Final Bid – $2,250**
- Lemony Snicket—Winner gets his/her name uttered (not necessarily correctly pronounced) in the thirteenth book in his Unfortunate Events series. **Final Bid – $6,300**
- Nora Roberts—Winner gets a character named after him/her in a book released in the spring of 2006. **Final Bid – $6,844.69**

★ ★ ★ ★ ★

THE YELLOW BADGE OF COURAGE

After pledging Delta Upsilon fraternity in 1890 as a freshman at Lafayette University, Stephen Crane had no clue what was coming next. When a group of older brothers ripe for hazing came pounding on his door the following week, he was terrified and refused to let them in. All in good fun, they kicked down the door—but then stopped in their tracks. Crane was standing in the corner of his room, in his nightgown, with a revolver pointed straight at them. Crane may have thought he was getting robbed, but when the evening was settled he was hazed no more. No brother would mess with him again, but it didn't really matter. He had flunked out of school by Christmas break.

★ ★ ★ ★ ★

KIPLING'S GREAT DEPRESSION

When the apostle Paul said that the love of money was the root of all evil, author **Rudyard Kipling should have taken the warning a little more seriously.** While honeymooning with his new bride, Caroline Balestier, in 1892, the unthinkable happened—his bank failed. Unable to finish the romantic vacation, the couple had to cash out their travel tickets to get back home. Unfortunately, the money only got them as far as Vermont, the home state of most of Caroline's family. Instead of trying to continue on their way, they made the most of the situation and settled down in a dark green house Kipling nicknamed his "ship."

TALES OF THE RUDE AND CRUDE

A native of Bombay, India, Rudyard Kipling was only six years old when his parents took him to England and abandoned him at a foster home.

59

★ ★ ★ ★ ★

THE BROTHERS GRIMACE

The year 1812 was a bad year for Jakob and Wilhelm Grimm. They were so poor that they ate a single meal a day, which explains why so many of the characters in their famous tales suffered from hunger (think Hansel and Gretel). If that weren't enough, the Brothers Grimm were not comfortable with going down in history as children's authors. They viewed themselves as folklorists preserving German oral tradition. In fact, original versions of their stories were much darker than after Disney turned them into feel-good animated films. For example:

• In *Snow White*, the evil stepmother dies after being forced to dance around in red-hot iron shoes.

DID YOU KNOW

Grimms' Fairy Tales have been translated into more than 160 languages and are most popular in Japan, where there are two theme parks inspired by the literature.

- In *The Goose Maid*, one of the servants is stripped down, shoved into a barrel of sharp nails, and then rolled down the street.

- In *The Frog King*, the princess does not kiss the frog—she throws him at the wall because it was so ugly. Once it bounced to the floor, it awoke as a prince.

★ ★ ★ ★ ★

PLAGIARISM OF JURASSIC PROPORTIONS

A Chicago native, Michael Crichton graduated summa cum laude from Harvard University and later received an M.D. from Harvard Medical School. So why would a man with such an esteemed education have the originality of his work questioned in court? Crichton was once summoned to trial to deny accusations that he plagiarized the film *Twister* (another screenwriter claimed that Crichton had stolen it from his version, entitled *Catch the Wind*). Although he defended that specific film while on the stand, Crichton did own up to the fact that he had plagiarized in the past—while a student at Harvard. One of his professors had been giving him unusually low grades, and to prove to another school authority that there was bias, Crichton submitted a paper by *1984* author George Orwell with his own name on it. He actually received a B- and told the jury that he never intended to give the school a bad name.

CHEESY MOMENTS OF CONTROVERSY

In 2003, Michael Crichton gave the unusual and controversial lecture "Aliens Cause Global Warming" while a guest of honor at the California Institute of Technology. He explained to students his theory of "junk science," which he believes is propaganda such as nuclear winters, global warming, and the dangers of secondhand smoke. He asserted that the belief in these theories, like the belief in aliens, is not proven scientific fact but a matter of faith.

★ ★ ★ ★ ★

SUCKING UP IN THE SLAMMER

The *Call Of The Wild* author **Jack London found himself in trouble with the law a few times in his life.** He had stolen things from orchards and hopped trains in the past—but when he was arrested for vagrancy in Buffalo, New York, at just eighteen years old, he couldn't believe it. Just visiting as a tourist, London was sentenced thirty days in jail. He wasn't even allowed to speak up for himself and claim his rights as an American citizen. Later, when he wrote *The Road*, he made public all the bizarre things that happened to him behind bars. He actually befriended a prison hand who, in exchange for small talk, got him a posh job as a hall monitor of sorts. Because he was on the warden's good side, London made

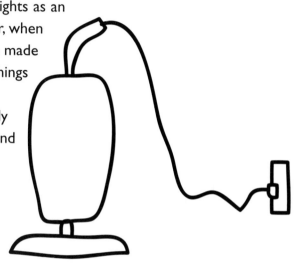

other friends who expected him to use his connections to help them organize crime upon their release—but London wouldn't have anything to do with it. He ran from the other ex-cons by hopping a freight train and never looked back.

★ ★ ★ ★ ★

HOMETOWN HORROR

The controversial author of the 2000 remake *American Psycho*, **Bret Easton Ellis is from a hometown with a reputation nearly as scary as his movie.** In December 2004, a ten-year-old boy named Ashton Allen disappeared from Midland, Texas. Just one month prior, Ellis'

In April 1991, *Rolling Thunder Magazine* published an interview with Bret Easton Ellis titled "Mamas, Don't Let Your Babies Grow Up to be Literary Rock Stars."

nine-year-old son Robby had disappeared, as well. The two families were neighbors, and authorities expected the disappearances to be related to a string of other vanishings in the area. In an attempt to figure out what had happened to his son, who he had with actress Jayne Dennis, Ellis uncovered a series of Instant Message conversations Allen had had with the other missing boys. However, once a variety of websites got a hold of the conversations, they used them to make it look like all of the boys were unhappy at home and planned to run away together. Ellis was also derided as an unfit source because of his history with illegal substances and dreaming up "horrific scenarios" for a living. The case has not been solved to this day.

★ ★ ★ ★ ★

FIRED FOR BEING FRANK

Deliverance author **James Dickey marked his worst day ever in 1955**, while serving as a creative writing teacher at the University of Florida. Dickey had tired of his job and decided he would really rather focus on poetry. He didn't intend to quit right away, but he soon embarrassed the school enough to earn himself a pink slip. While speaking in front of faculty wives and influential women from around Gainesville, he read a poem he had written titled "The Father's Body," which describes how a young boy begins to notice the differences in sexual maturity between himself and his father. The women were appalled, and when Dickey refused to issue an apology, he was sent packing.

James Dickey played wingback during Clemson College's fall game against rival University of Carolina in 1942. The sport distracted him so much from his studies that when he was drafted into World War II, he was failing all but one class. When he returned from war a poet, his teachers were shocked and impressed.

DID YOU KNOW

In the mid-1950s, James Dickey wrote advertising copy for Coca-Cola and Lays Potato Chips.

★ ★ ★ ★ ★

TALL TALES AND NECK NAILS

Along with a group of friends who were also young writers, *Frankenstein's* **Mary Shelley set out to organize a ghost-story writing contest** in the 1800s. They were all so captivated by the frightening tales they had read in the book *Fantasmagoriana* that they wanted to create similar stories. Although one of Shelley's friends, Dr. John Polidori, came up with *The Vampyre*—which would later influence Bram Stoker as he wrote *Dracula*—Shelley couldn't come up with a thing. However, the following night she had a terrifying dream that inspired one of the most famous pieces of science-fiction literature in history. Shelley saw an image of a student kneeling beside some creature he had made. When she woke up, she put the story on paper. It would later evolve into *Frankenstein*—a piece that lasted long after her friends' silly tales.

LOVE'S LITTLE SURPRISES

Mary Shelley's husband, Percy, believed in free love and tried to "share" her with his friend, Thomas Hogg. She, like Percy's first wife, refused the offer.

★ ★ ★ ★ ★

A WRECK MADE HIM A WRECK

He may be famous for writing about space travel, but *Fahrenheit 451* author **Ray Bradbury's imaginative courage was challenged forever when he witnessed a gruesome car accident** as a boy. He may have grown up to write about travel, but thanks to the fear the image instilled in his life, he has never once driven a car. Not only automobiles scare him either—he did not set foot on an airplane until he was sixty-two, with the exception of a ride in the Goodyear Blimp two decades before.

★ ★ ★ ★ ★

A FASHION POLICE NIGHTMARE

Oscar Wilde had one thing in life more frightening than anything else—his hideous floral wallpaper. Author of the famed 1891 *The Picture of Dorian Gray*, Wilde joked to a friend while on his deathbed: "My wallpaper and I are fighting a duel to the death. One or the other of us has to go." The witty statement became so famous that the Paris hotel where he was staying at the time left that same wallpaper up in the first-floor room for the next one hundred years. It wasn't replaced until 2000, when it was covered with blue-green frescos to match the rest of the hotel.

★ ★ ★ ★ ★

Snored Stiff

Some people say there's nothing a good night's sleep can't cure. J.R.R. Tolkien hated those people—**he spent most of his marriage sleeping in a different room than his wife**, because she couldn't stand his snoring. Mrs. Tolkien called dibs on the bedroom, while he had to settle for snoozing in the bathroom/dressing room. Each morning he could wake up and hop into the bathtub without even leaving the room. Not much of a morning person, Tolkien was known to stumble around the house at an ungodly hour to get his two youngest boys up for mass. His greatest feat each day—trying not to trip over their toy trains.

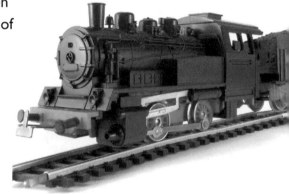

Like most boys, his sons were train fanatics—but Tolkien just didn't get it. To him, trains represented everything noisy and dirty, but he put up with the toys and tried not to stub his toe while wiping the sleep out of his eyes.

★ ★ ★ ★ ★

A TIME (NOT) TO KILL

Although he was as much of a womanizer as his classy protagonist James Bond, author Ian Fleming lacked courage. While working for the Naval Intelligence Division during the war, Fleming volunteered to go through espionage training. While learning how to assassinate someone, however, he lost his nerve and failed for not being able to pull the trigger.

Ian Flemming wrote *Casino Royale* and his other famed James Bond books in Jamaica, in a house he called Goldeneye, where he wouldn't be distracted by busy London life. He awoke at 7:30 a.m., went skinny-dipping in the ocean, ate scrambled eggs, laid in the sun, and then got to work.

★ ★ ★ ★ ★

DEATH BE NOT PROUD (OR QUICK)

Famous for his pessimistic tale *Heart of Darkness*, author **Joseph Conrad had a fear of imminent death after marrying his wife,** Jessie George, in 1896. Before he proposed to her, he even explained that he didn't think he had long to live and that he had "no intention of having children." His anxiety was needless—he lived 28 more years, to the ripe old age of 67.

★ ★ ★ ★ ★

A SHARK'S SWEET REVENGE

The original author of *Jaws*, **Peter Benchley had a fearful realization as he swam about in a shark cage** off the coast of Australia in 2000—"What if the sharks got back at me for giving them such a bad reputation?" The comment was only a half-fear of his, he said, adding that if he had started the book later than he did, he wouldn't have been able to write it. Why? Because in the 1970s, sharks were known as ruthless killers who stalked the oceans for human feasts. Today some scientists maintain that Great White shark aggression is simply curiosity, not vengeance.

Peter Benchley was nearly killed by a shark when he got caught in a fisherman's line while swimming in the Bahamas after writing Jaws. He was filming a television program about ocean life. A shark grabbed the stick that was attached to his wrist and dragged him through the water.

Regardless, Benchley's book caused a lot of people to panic and go out hunting for their own sharks to kill. Laughing that he could never have predicted how his fans would react to Jaws, Benchley compared

70

the situation to a date he had in 1961—"When I went to see Psycho ... my date wet her pants. I cannot be responsible for how people react."

★ ★ ★ ★ ★

ALONG CAME A FAILURE

The brainchild of American writer James Patterson, *Along Came A Spider* should have been a hugely successful thriller when it was made into a movie in 2001. However, when the film opened at the box office, and movie critics at CNN put their fingers to their keyboards, the day proved a bad one for the story's original author. Although billed as a "psychological suspense thriller" with big name actors such as Morgan Freeman, the film flopped. Critics noted that the villain's motive was foolish, several of Patterson's plot lines had been cut out, and the script was completely illogical. Patterson spent the rest of the week hoping his fans picked up *his* version—the book—and stayed away from the theatres. He could finally relate to best-selling author John LeCarré, who once said, "Having your book turned into a movie is like seeing your oxen turned into bouillon cubes."

★ ★ ★ ★ ★

HALLOWEEN HUMILIATION

The writer of such creative sci-fi works as *The Whores of Babylon, Ian Watson's jaw hit the floor when he arrived at the British National Science Fiction Convention in 2005. The staff had decided to

have a little fun with each
attendee by assigning
them secret identities.
Watson's costume was a
tall, curly wig, tight pants,
and a silver sword. His
character? Inigo Montoya
from *The Princess Bride*.
Despite looking strikingly
similar to Captain Hook,
Watson spent the entire evening

faking a laugh to cheesy lines such as, "You killed my father. Prepare to
die!" At least he won the award for best costume.

CLEAR AND PRESENT DANGER (ON YOUR LAWN)

**Tom Clancy lives in
a fifteen thousand-
square-foot mansion**
with a half-mile driveway,
basketball courts, tennis
courts, and a football field. His home has twenty-four rooms,
sixteen-foot ceilings, four computers, seven TVs, an indoor swimming
pool, and a pistol range. So what could his wife possibly get him for
Christmas as a surprise? A yard ornament that would scare him and

then make him wet his pants with excitement—his very own World War II tank. Clancy may have thought he was living one of his own plotlines for a brief second, but after he realized the tank was all his, he jumped for joy.

★ ★ ★ ★ ★

GONE WITHOUT A TRACE

Ambrose Bierce wrote a lot about war,
but he never envisioned he would get caught up in one himself. In October 1913, the seventy-something writer decided to take a leisurely trip visiting old Civil War battlefields. A few months later, he

had been through both Louisiana and Texas—but to get there he had to drive through warn-torn El Paso, which was teeming with revolutionaries at the time. Curious as always, he joined a small

villa's army to scope out the situation. However, he must have gotten more caught up in the action than intended, because once the group got to Chihuahua, Bierce was nowhere to be found. The last recorded proof of his existence was a letter he wrote to a friend on December 26. His disappearance remains a mystery to this day. Could Bierce have known of his imminent fate? Maybe. Not long before he vanished, Bierce wrote in a letter, "Good-by—if you hear of my being stood up against a Mexican stone wall and shot to rags please know that I think that a pretty good way to depart this life. It beats old age, disease, or falling down the cellar stairs. To be a Gringo in Mexico—ah, that is euthanasia."

★ ★ ★ ★ ★

Panic and Practical Jokes

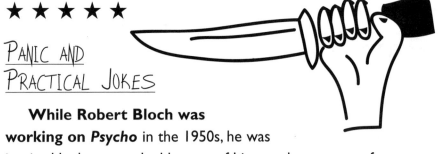

While Robert Bloch was working on *Psycho* in the 1950s, he was inspired by how spooked he was of his own hometown of Weyauwega, Wisconsin. Serial killer Ed Gein was on the prowl, and many people in the city feared that any neighbor could be the monster they had heard so much about. Bloch always had the killer in the back of his mind, and after he wrote the book he realized that his own antagonist greatly resembled Gein's crimes and motivation.

Bloch may have been freaked out, but he wasn't so scared he couldn't have a little fun on set. One day, he took the prop he was using for the mother's corpse and put it in actress Janet Leigh's dressing room. He judged how scary it was by the loudness of her scream.

THREE THINGS YOU NEVER KNEW ABOUT... PSYCHO

- When the book was made into a movie, it was the first film to kill off its only main character halfway into the plotline. Viewers had no clue where the story would go from there.

- It was the first movie to show a toilet flushed onscreen.

- It was rumored that Alfred Hitchcock made the water in the shower ice cold so his actress' scream would be genuine. However this was denied on several occasions. In fact, the water was so warm that the coverings used to hide her body accidentally started peeling off during filming.

Chapter 4

Off Their Rockers: Famous Poets Gone Loony

Off Their Rockers: Famous Poets Gone Loony

"Crazy" can manifest itself in a number of ways. There's the babbling fool who talks himself into the grave. There's the impatient idiot who destroys a world-class poem after one bad critique. There's the arrogant loser who turns down the Nobel Prize because his feelings got hurt. Whether they were loony enough to be institutionalized or simply had a screw loose, when it came to making judgment calls, these writers led lives just as odd and unpredictable as their poetry.

DID YOU KNOW

As a senior in high school, Kenneth Fearing was voted wittiest boy and class pessimist.

★ ★ ★ ★ ★

THE MYSTERIOUS MUMBLER: EDGAR ALLAN POE

If marrying your thirteen-year-old cousin isn't enough of a red flag to prove you are nuts, then running around the streets of Baltimore in a panic attack—while wearing another man's clothes—should be. Edgar Allan Poe did both. On October 3, 1849, he was found wandering, delirious and incoherent. He spent the next several days in and out of consciousness at Washington College Hospital and never got the chance to explain the episode before he died four days later. Unfortunately, Poe's physicians and acquaintances from that night never agreed on a cause of death. Some said he had gotten miserably drunk, while others argued that they never smelled liquor on his breath.
Every possible condition—from brain disease and diabetes to rabies and syphilis—was considered, but the true tale of his demise may never be known.

DID YOU KNOW

At age forty, Edgar Allan Poe was one of the youngest American writers to die during the nineteenth century. Only Sidney Lanier and Stephen Crane died younger.

★ ★ ★ ★ ★

THE TEASING TEACHER: ANNE SEXTON

Anne Sexton loved to get her crowd a little anxious before she did poetry readings. She would purposefully show up ten minutes late. When she arrived, she would mosey over to the microphone, light a cigarette, and greet them with a pithy line—"I am going to read a poem that tells you what kind of poet I am, what kind of woman I am, so if you don't like it, you can leave." However, the kind of woman Sexton was was anything but graceful—she suffered from suicidal thoughts and often admitted to hating herself. Even as a child she had thoughts about death. When her boyfriend was late for a date one winter morning, he found her motionless in the snow with what looked like blood on her head. He panicked, but she thought it was a good joke.

Addicted to sleeping pills, Sexton spent some time in mental institutions before committing suicide in 1974. Her female fans could relate to her dissatisfaction with being a housewife and a woman in the 1960s.

★ ★ ★ ★ ★

THE SILLY DRUNK: DYLAN THOMAS

Twentieth-century Welsh poet **Dylan Thomas had a little love affair with liquor**. Known as one of the most exciting, theatrical writers of his day, he would often tour the country to visit his admirers. After one rowdy night in a New York City bar called the White Horse Tavern, however, Thomas suddenly collapsed and died. Although many believed the man drank himself to death, official records claimed it was actually pneumonia that did him in. Regardless, Thomas's last words were recorded as "I've had 18 straight whiskeys; I think this is a record!"

MYSTERIOUS MYTHS

Some music buffs report that songwriter Bob Dylan, born Robert Allen Zimmerman, changed his name as a tribute to writer Dylan Thomas. However, the musician has always insisted the claim is not true.

THE ANXIOUS BRIDE: SARA TEASDALE

After ignoring a sudden bout of cold feet before walking down the aisle, poet Sara Teasdale decided that her marriage to Ernst Filsinger was nothing like she imagined. Although she never told him, just moments after she accepted his proposal she sat alone, terrified that she had given him the wrong answer. What would this mean for her poetry? She also had an old lover from a summer fling who wrote letters to her, begging her not to marry another. If that weren't enough, once they were married Sara insisted she and her young husband have separate bedrooms. She had always had her privacy, she said, and feared she could not rest with someone else lingering about. The couple divorced shortly after their fifteenth anniversary.

THE PRIDEFUL PIMP: LORD BYRON

In the early 1800s, Lord Byron was living large in the luxurious four-floor Palazzo Mocenigo in Venice, Italy. He had fourteen servants and dedicated an entire floor of his home to his pets, which included a variety of dogs and monkeys. His affection for women was even greater, though, and the rest of his spacious home accommodated a long list of Venetian lovers. Byron was so promiscuous that rumors of his relationships spread as far as England. His daily routine: sleep late, take an afternoon ride on one of his horses, sleep with his women, and then write late into the night.

LOVE'S LITTLE SURPRISES

Lord Byron once boasted that he had sex with more than 250 women in Venice in only one year.

★ ★ ★ ★ ★

THE OVERREACTOR: SIR WALTER SCOTT

Paranoid about whether or not his work was up to par, Sir Walter Scott was a little misled when he received criticisms of his first serious poems. After reading a few stanzas to some friends who gave him very few compliments in return, he threw a fit and tossed the manuscript into a fire. Once he realized that he had overreacted and his buddies were actually interested in his continuing the piece for publication, he panicked and had to write it over again. Six weeks (and many late nights) later, "The Lay of the Last Minstrel" was complete.

★ ★ ★ ★ ★

DOOMED BY HIMSELF: JOHN DONNE

Long known for his beautiful stanzas and Christian sermons, John Donne was a charmer. However, not many people know that he may have predicted his own death. While ill in 1631, his thoughts constantly turned to the grave. In what ended up being his last speech from the pulpit, Donne delivered what sounded like his own eulogy. During that time, merely weeks before his death, Donne even had his portrait made while wearing the shroud in which he wanted to be buried.

> ### TALES OF THE RUDE AND CRUDE
> John Donne's brother was imprisoned, where he died of a fever, for protecting a priest. His uncle, a Jesuit, was hanged, drawn, and quartered for his faith.

★ ★ ★ ★ ★

THE DATE WHO WAS DUMPED: ROBERT FROST

While a college student, Robert Frost published a short book of poems called *Twilight* for his girlfriend, Elinor White, who was studying at Saint Lawrence University in New York. He printed only two copies and made a special trip to New York to present her with the special gift. However, Elinor took the book and said goodbye

SLUGGISH IN SCHOOL

Robert Frost received more than forty honorary degrees in his lifetime, but he never bothered to actually earn one. He dropped out of Dartmouth College after only one semester and quit Harvard after less than two years. He never trusted what he called "academic knowledge."

without sticking around to talk about it. It upset Frost so much that he destroyed his own copy. The one remaining copy of *Twilight* is one of the most valuable collectibles in the publishing industry.

★ ★ ★ ★ ★

THE THIRD WHEEL: EZRA POUND

American poet and critic Ezra Pound may have been a dazzling influence to classic writers such as Ernest Hemmingway and Robert Frost, but his reputation for being a little nutty only increased with age. In 1922, Pound and his wife, Dorothy Shakespear, added a third-party to their relationship—violinist Olga Rudge. The three of them remained "committed" until the end of Pound's life. After World War I, he faced charges of treason but was dismissed for being insane, so instead of jail time he was simply moved to St.

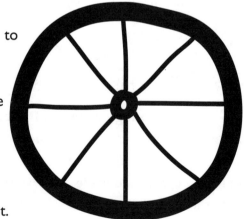

Elizabeth's Hospital in Washington, D.C. For the next twelve years, Pound passed the time in his padded, white-wall rooms writing books, enjoying conjugal visits with a number of female visitors, and communicating with the States' Rights Democratic Party about his strategies to continue racial segregation in the South.

★ ★ ★ ★ ★

THE PAINFUL PRESCRIPTION: LORD TENNYSON

The master behind "Sir Launcelot and Queen Guinevere," **Lord Tennyson came down with what he called a bad cold in 1845**—but he didn't go to a regular doctor. Instead, he put himself up in a mental institution that promised to cure his "symptoms." There he was denied reading, sitting near a fire, and sipping tea and coffee. He had to lie on wet sheets all day long and get up only to alternate between icy baths and steaming showers. Tennyson's

TALES OF THE RUDE AND CRUDE

Lord Tennyson once wrote a poem about Poland that was hundreds of lines long, but one of his maids accidentally used it as fodder for a fire.

caretakers promised that "severe cold water treatment" combined with avoiding alcohol and rich foods would cause his body to expel whatever toxins were making him sick. Of course, this was through vomiting and diarrhea.

★ ★ ★ ★ ★

THE ANNOYING ACQUAINTANCE: WALT WHITMAN

Accustomed to the flexible life he led in the woods while writing *Leaves of Grass*, **poet Walt Whitman was a bit of a nuisance later in life** when it came to being a houseguest. Partially crippled from a stroke, he was cared for by his brother (George Washington Whitman) and his wife, Louisa, in Camden. However, when Louisa would ring the dinner bell, Whitman would ignore it. Instead of coming down for the meal, she would find him splashing around in the bathtub singing "The Star Spangled Banner," "When Johnny Comes Marching Home," or an array of Italian operas. She would find him leashing his yellow and white dog, Tip, for a walk. She would find him asleep in his room. There was no way to get

> "I celebrate myself, and sing myself."
> — Walt Whitman

Whitman to comply with a firm schedule. In fact, he was so stubborn that he even refused book offers simply because they hadn't been his idea or they wouldn't work well with his lazy daily life.

★ ★ ★ ★ ★

THE GRUDGE MATCH MASTER: BORIS PASTERNAK

When authors are awarded the Nobel Prize for Literature, they are rarely crazy enough to say "no thanks" and return the checks. However, Boris Pasternak did just that. He was proud of his work on *Doctor Zhivago*— the main character, whose surname means "live" in Russian, was supposed to represent the author's love for life. But Pasternak turned bitter when he couldn't find a single publisher to accept the work in his home country. He had to smuggle it to Italy for its 1957 release, and even then the Soviet Union waged a wide-scale campaign against it. When he was awarded the Nobel Prize in 1958, he declined to accept it. Not until 1987 was *Doctor Zhivago* finally published in the USSR.

THREE THINGS YOU NEVER KNEW ABOUT … BORIS PASTERNAK

- He worked at a chemical factory during World War I.

- He wrote a poetry collection titled *My Sister Life* after falling in love with a young Jewish girl, but he was too embarrassed to have it published for four years.

- After he wrote a collection of poems titled *The Second Birth*, his colleagues described him as "Emily Dickinson in trousers."

★ ★ ★ ★ ★

THE THREE-RING CIRCUS: W.H. AUDEN

While working on a book of poems for a publishing company in the early 1940s, W.H. Auden paid $25 a month to

rent a bedroom and living room in the top floor of a boarding house. He had high hopes for intelligent, highbrow roommates with whom he could share deep discussions and lines from his poetry. One roomie did turn out to be *The Heart is a Lonely Hunter* novelist Carson McCullers—however, the rest of them belonged in the loony bin. The circus-like atmosphere included a chimpanzee and a man who could puff a cigarette with his rear end. However, Auden was happy living there and eventually deemed himself "House Pop." He insisted that everyone arrive for meals on time, dismiss their guests before 1:00 a.m., and stick to just a few squares of toilet paper when they used the bathroom. He may have been a little pushy—especially when he found out the other boarders were stealing his cigarettes—but he sincerely cared about each and every one of them.

★ ★ ★ ★ ★

PANICKED AND PARANOID: ROBERT BURNS

When Scottish poet Robert Burns was a boy, his mother had a maid named Betty Davis who would fill his imagination with tall tales of witches, fairies, ghosts, giants, and dragons. While Davis probably thought the bedtime stories were all in good fun, Burns was actually paranoid for years, peeking around corners and over his shoulders for the monsters he had heard about so many years earlier. In addition to his preoccupation with fear, by the time he was a teenager, Burns was a hypochondriac.

★ ★ ★ ★ ★

THE SECRET BRIDE: ELIZABETH BARRETT BROWNING

Elizabeth Barrett Browning, poet and lover of writer Robert Browning, **counted down the days until she and her fiancé were wed.** Though the seriousness of their relationship was a secret, she kept detailed notes about their love. Elizabeth was so careful to keep the truth about their "friendship" from her family that her ninety-first meeting with Robert (recorded in her diary as such) was the first time they saw each other outside of her father's house. It was also their wedding day. As she made up a tale to her parents and snuck away to elope, she was so nervous that she fainted and had to be dragged into a chemist's shop to be revived. Not long after Elizabeth said her "I do's," she had to head back to her father's home. It was weeks before anyone found out they had married.

★ ★ ★ ★ ★

TROUBLE WITH TWINS: KATHERINE MANSFIELD

When short-story-writer-turned-poet Katherine Mansfield moved to Europe for the first time as an adult (at twenty years old) in 1908, she was a rebellious, crazy wreck. Within ten months of living there, she had already borne an illegitimate child, divorced a lover after less than twenty-four hours of marriage, dappled with drugs, and suffered a miscarriage. She was so wild that when her childhood love, Arnold, wrote her a letter saying that they no longer had a future together, she reacted like any crazed woman would do and moved on to a new love—Arnold's twin brother, Garnet.

★ ★ ★ ★ ★

Mama's Boy Mayhem: Kenneth Fearing

"Angel Arm" (1929) poet Kenneth Fearing was too stubborn to develop a good work ethic. He couldn't keep a nine-to-five job for more than a few months until after his fiftieth birthday. His work history is rumored to have included short spurts as a journalist, a mill hand, a pants salesman, and a lumberjack. When his wife, Rachel, had a baby in the 1930s, however, Kenneth's mother forced his non-committal attitude to an end. She stopped giving him his $15/month allowance and insisted he start accepting his responsibilities as a father. From then on, he did his best to put bread on the table.

★ ★ ★ ★ ★

Inspired By Visions: Vachel Lindsay

Made most famous by his poem "Euclid," **Vachel Lindsay started a habit of writing in a diary when he was just seven years old.** While the hobby isn't much to write home about, what was odd was that Lindsay labeled each notebook with the phrase "This Book Belongs to Christ." He claimed to have had visions of the Old Testament prophets twice and saw his poems as a way to spread "the gospel of beauty." He may have taken

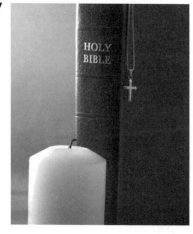

his religious vows a little too far, though. He was so naïve (and so afraid of what his father threatened to do to him if he ever had sex) that he never formed serious relationships with women beyond idealized infatuations.

★ ★ ★ ★ ★

FOLLOWING IN LOONY FOOTSTEPS: CHARLOTTE MEW

English poet Charlotte Mew was doomed to a life of bad, crazy luck. Born in London to an architect who died early in his career, Mew had two siblings institutionalized for mental illness. Fearing a similar fate, Charlotte and her sister Anne vowed never to get married—they couldn't bear the thought of possibly passing on a recessive gene to children. Unfortunately, Anne died. Mew became severely depressed and was admitted into a nursing home, where she killed herself by swallowing disinfectant.

Chapter 5

Authors' Hall of Shame: Most Embarrassing Moments

Authors' Hall of Shame: Most Embarrassing Moments

Everyone has moments of incredible shame—those defining incidents when all eyes are on you ... and you'd give anything to take back the silly thing you just said or did. You thought tripping down the stairs in high school was bad enough, but wait until you hear these tales of blushing blunders from across the literary globe.

CHEESY MOMENTS OF CONTROVERSY

When he was just fifteen years old, Leo Tolstoy's brothers took him to a brothel for his first sexual experience with a woman. Although initially plagued with guilt, he eventually became promiscuous and contracted gonorrhea.

★ ★ ★ ★ ★

I DRINK YOU'VE HAD TOO MUCH TO THINK

The Culprit: William Faulkner

Why He's Blushing:
He got tipsy before
giving one of the most
important speeches of
his life.

**The Rest of the
Story:** Faulkner has
long been known for his
challenging works, but
when he got drunk
before giving an
acceptance speech at the
1949 Nobel Prize
awards, his words were
more confusing than ever. His nephew knew he was prone to binging
before big events and tried to trick him into staying sober, but as
soon as Faulkner found out he was setting sail for Stockholm, he
tipped up the bottle and didn't look back. He mumbled his inebriated
speech, and stood way too far away from the microphone for anyone
to hear what he had to say. Not until the public read the printed
version of the speech could they decide whether it was even worthy
of applause.

DID YOU KNOW

Although his true motives are unknown, some suspect that William Faulkner changed the spelling of his name from Falkner to Faulkner to make him sound like more of a British aristocrat when he entered the Royal Air Force as a young man. Others believe it was simply to make it easier to spell.

★ ★ ★ ★ ★

PRETTY IN PINK

The Culprit: Ernest Hemingway's parents

Why He's Blushing: His mother tried to pass him off as a girl.

The Rest of the Story: You know it's going to be a hard life when you spend your childhood dressed as the opposite sex. Ernest Hemmingway's mother wanted twin girls so

THREE THINGS YOU NEVER KNEW ABOUT... ERNEST HEMINGWAY

- He began his career as a seventeen-year-old reporter for *The Kansas City Star* in 1916.
- He wrote *The Sun Also Rises* (1926) in around six weeks from his favorite Paris restaurant, La Closerie des Lilas.
- Several members of his family committed suicide including his father, both of his siblings, and himself.

much that when he was born in 1899, she tricked the town by dressing him just like his sister, who was eighteen months older. She paraded them around with similar haircuts and identical clothing, hoping her peers would believe the children to be twins. In public, she even referred to Hemingway as Ernestine instead of Ernest.

★ ★ ★ ★ ★

FAME AND FROSTBITE

The Culprit: Francis Bacon

Why He's Blushing: He killed himself with his best idea yet.

The Rest of the Story: One would assume that Francis Bacon, one of the most famous philosophers of the seventeenth century, would have enough

street smarts not to freeze to death. However, while driving home one winter day he had a brilliant idea—why not preserve his groceries with snow? As he rushed off to stuff his chickens with icy slush, Bacon got a little over zealous. By the time he was finished, he had contracted a severe case of pneumonia. He died less than a month later. The one thing he got out of the deal—he didn't have to pay his £22,000 debt.

> "Hope is a good breakfast, but it is a bad supper." – Francis Bacon

★ ★ ★ ★ ★

SONNETS AND SHOTGUN WEDDINGS

The Culprit: William Shakespeare

Why He's Blushing: Bullies spread rumors that he hinted at homosexuality in his writing.

The Rest of the Story: Shakespeare was an easy target for jokes when it came to his love life. He was

101

OTHER AUTHORS WITH A THING FOR THE SAME SEX

William Shakespeare wasn't the only writer to be accused of being bisexual or homosexual. HERE'S A LIST ...

- Emily Dickinson—Although often portrayed as a recluse, she frequently wrote letters to a schoolteacher named Susan Gilbert. Dickinson's family threw most of Gilbert's old letters to their daughter into the fireplace once they discovered the collection after her death, but Dickinson's letters to Gilbert still remain. In one letter she wrote: "Sweet Hour, blessed Hour, to carry me to you ... long enough to snatch one kiss, and whisper Good bye, again."

- Bret Easton Ellis—Born in Los Angeles, this *Rules of Attraction* novelist was bisexual for most of his life but refused to publicly admit it until 2005, when he told *The New York Times* that his partner had died at the age of thirty.

- Oscar Wilde
- Tennessee Williams
- A.E. Housman
- Allen Ginsberg
- Willa Cather
- Carson McCullers
- Adrienne Rich
- Fannie Flagg

- Gore Vidal
- Edward Albee
- Marcel Proust
- Andre Gide
- Amy Lowell
- Edna St. Vincent Millay
- Sara Teasdale
- Virginia Woolf

rumored to have married Anne Hathaway when she was already three months pregnant, and his reputation among both women and men forever changed once critics read his works. Twenty-six of his sonnets appeared to be love poems to a married woman, referred to as the Dark Lady, and another 126 are addressed to a man, Fair Lord. Although Elizabethans commonly referred to their friendships as more aggressive types of love in poetry, critics believed Shakespeare was actually referring to sexual rendezvous. Some argue that the "speaker" in the poems does not necessarily have to be Shakespeare; he could have been writing in third person. Others disagree and insist he was indeed bisexual.

★ ★ ★ ★ ★

A GREAT GETS HIS HOPES UP

The Culprit: Truman Capote

Why He's Blushing: He promised buddies his latest story would be printed in one of the country's most popular magazines—but it never was.

The Rest of the Story: *Breakfast at Tiffany's* was originally supposed to be printed as a fictional article in *Harper's Bazaar* magazine in the 1950s—but at the last minute, *after* the magazine requested some of Capote's raffish language be changed and had it laid out to be printed, the editors changed their minds. Embarrassed and outraged at the broken contract, Capote announced that the magazine had stopped running "quality fiction" for their readers. He later sold the manuscript to *Esquire* and Random House Publishing.

DID YOU KNOW

Truman Capote got the title *Breakfast at Tiffany's* from a story he once heard about a young Marine in World War II. The man's friend offered to take him to breakfast, but it was Sunday and the shops were closed. "Where would you like to go? Pick the fanciest, most expensive place in town," he said. The Marine's reply, "Let's have breakfast at Tiffany's."

★ ★ ★ ★ ★

DREAMING UP DIRT

The Culprit: Mitch Albom

Why He's Blushing: He "used his imagination" in what should have been hard news.

The Rest of the Story: Author of the popular *Tuesdays with Morrie* and *The Five People You'll Meet in Heaven*, Mitch Albom hasn't always been the reflective literary giant most believe him to be. A graduate of Brandeis and Columbia Universities, he was disciplined while working as a journalist at the *Detroit Free Press* for allegedly fabricating information in one of his stories. He assured readers that two former Spartan basketball players would attend a Final Four game – but they never showed up. Albom's harshest critics called for him to be fired, and he has been trying to live the scandal down ever since.

★ ★ ★ ★ ★

Oh Sally ... I Mean Sonya

The Culprit: Leo Tolstoy

Why He's Blushing: He bragged about past lovers on his wedding night.

The Rest of the Story: Lonely and in desperate need of a bride, Leo Tolstoy broke down one New Year's Day and vowed that

if he did not get married by the end of 1859, he would count himself a bachelor forever. It didn't happen, but he did eventually marry three years later. However, Tolstoy put a damper on their marital bliss with an odd request on the wedding night—he insisted his new bride, Sonya, read all of his old diaries, which included details about his past relationships with other women. Tolstoy may have simply wanted to dispel all secrets, but Sonya was disgusted. The day after the wedding, she wrote in her own diary about her jealousy and the "filth" to which she had been subjected.

"I clearly realized that my biography, if it suppressed all the nastiness and criminality of my life—as they customarily write biographies—would be a lie, and that if one is going to write my biography, one must write the whole truth."—Leo Tolstoy

★ ★ ★ ★ ★

PINING FOR A PRENUP

The Culprit: Tom Clancy

Why He's Blushing: His ex-wife took him for all he was worth.

The Rest of the Story: Espionage thrillers such as *Clear and Present Danger* may have put Tom Clancy on the literary map, but his trip up the corporate ladder came to a shrieking halt when his ex-wife got her share of

the divorce settlement in 1998. Clancy was making offers to purchase the Minnesota Vikings when the settlement came through and caused his net worth to plummet. Stories of an alleged affair with an assistant district attorney Clancy had met online reached the wrong ears, and the author could no longer afford the team.

★ ★ ★ ★ ★

A PRIEST WITH A PROBLEM

The Culprit: Horatio Alger

Why He's Blushing: He got caught "making friends" with little boys.

The Rest of the Story: Horatio Alger was one of the best-known nineteenth century American authors. He wrote more than 130 rags-to-riches dime novels such as *Ragged Dick* and *Luck and Pluck*. After being rejected from service during the Civil War because of his pesky asthma attacks, Alger decided to become a minister. Instead of preaching the word of God, however, he got personal with people way below the legal age limit. In 1866 he suddenly left his position at First Parish Unitarian Church of Brewster. It was later uncovered that he had been kicked out for initiating sexual relationships with several boys.

★ ★ ★ ★ ★

THE IMPORTANCE OF BEING BULLIED

The Culprit: Oscar Wilde

Why He's Blushing: He was beat up for being a sissy, then teased by his boyfriend's dad.

The Rest of the Story: Clues about Oscar Wilde's sexual orientation came early in life. In college, he rebelled against trends and wore his hair long; made fun of masculine sports; and decorated his room with china, sunflowers, and peacock feathers. He was not easily accepted by other students (he frequently had his room trashed and was dunked in a nearby river for being so odd), but he was not ashamed of his homosexual tendencies. Not yet, at least. His true embarrassment regarding his reputation would come later in life, when his boyfriend's father went to great lengths to break up the relationship. The 9th Marquess of Queensbury, he made shameless plans to throw

> ### LOVE'S LITTLE SURPRISES
> While in prison, Oscar Wilde wrote a 50,000-word letter to his boyfriend, Lord Alfred Douglas, which he wasn't allowed to send until he was released.

vegetables at Wilde while he was on stage and leave him calling cards referring to him as a sodomite. Wilde tried accusing him of criminal libel, but in court things just got worse. He actually admitted to lying while on the stand and ended up in court for "committing acts of gross indecency with other male persons."

★ ★ ★ ★ ★

SHOCKED STUPID

The Culprit: Paulo Coelho

Why He's Blushing: His parents gave him electro-shock therapy for misbehaving.

The Rest of the Story: Brazilian author Paulo Coelho, best known for his work on *The Alchemist*, had big plans for his future—that is, until his parents started bugging him about how much money he could make as an engineer. They strongly discouraged him from a literary life, but Coelho soon became rebellious and made a habit out of breaking the family rules. His plan backfired,

however, and his father decided that the only way to fix his son's attitude was to put him in a psych ward. At just seventeen years old, Coelho was locked up for what his dad called "signs of mental illness." The treatment—a few rounds of painful electroconvulsive therapy.

After he was released, the author became independent, joined a theater group, and got a job as a journalist. However, his peers had such a reputation of immorality that his parents, once again, threatened to send him back to the "hospital." He eventually was taken back, and when he got out, he became intensely withdrawn and depressed. On a hunch, his parents called for a second opinion from a different doctor who urged them to leave their son alone.

★ ★ ★ ★ ★

Family Controversy

The Culprit: Gertrude Franklin Horn Atherton

Why She's Blushing: Her book brought shame to her family.

The Rest of the Story: Born in San Fransisco, Atherton eloped at age nineteen and quickly had two children. However, her new hubby discouraged her love

for writing. The publication of her first novel, *The Randolphs of Redwoods* (1882), scandalized her family because of its feminism and sexual content. From then on she published other controversial works, such as *What Dreams May Come*, under a pseudonym.

★ ★ ★ ★ ★

THE PICKY EATER

The Culprit: Sherwood Anderson

Why He's Blushing: He died from swallowing a toothpick.

The Rest of the Story: Anderson was chewing on a toothpick after a meal in the early 1940s when suddenly—gulp—it slid right

> # DID YOU KNOW
> As a boy, Sherwood Anderson was nicknamed "Jobby" for working so many odd jobs to raise money for his family.

down his throat. At first he was probably amused, surprised that it actually made its way down to his stomach. But before long, the little sliver of wood took its revenge. As it passed through Anderson's intestines, the toothpick punctured the organ, causing an often fatal condition called peritonitis.

★ ★ ★ ★ ★

WE'RE OFF TO SEE THE UNEMPLOYMENT OFFICE ...

The Culprit: L. Frank Baum

Why He's Blushing: He did a crappy favor in hopes of a big break that never worked out.

The Rest of the Story:
He may be famous for his children's story *The Wonderful Wizard of Oz*, but L. Frank Baum had quite an embarrassing start to his theatrical career at age eighteen. A performing arts center duped him into revamping their stock of costumes in exchange for lead roles in their plays. However, the theater never came through on their end of the deal, and Baum never appeared front and center. Disappointed, he quit working there and instead took on a series of odd jobs, including breeding chickens and working as a clerk in his brother's-in-law dry goods company.

★ ★ ★ ★ ★

The Fashion of The Christ

The Culprit: James Kirkup

Why He's Blushing: He was sued for dishonoring Jesus Christ.

The Rest of the Story: James Kirkup thought he was being ingenious when he first wrote the famous poem "The Love That Dares To Speak Its Name"—especially when he got it published in the June 3, 1976, issue of *Gay News*. However, reader Mary Whitehouse wouldn't have such "filthy" rhymes pass by her eyes a second time. She was so offended, calling the poem "a blasphemous libel concerning the Christian religion," that she sued both the magazine and its publisher for allowing it to print. She wanted £7,763—paid by Gay News Ltd and the publisher. Kirkup was never involved in the settlement, but he was horrified that his piece would receive such a public flogging. *Gay News* couldn't care less about the fine, however—they raised a whopping £26,435 from the homosexual community to pay their dues, protect their right to free speech, and still have money leftover for pizza. Only one question remained—why was a pious Ms. Whitehouse flipping through the latest issue of *Gay News*?

★ ★ ★ ★ ★

HIGH SCHOOL HERESY

The Culprit: John Ashbery

Why He's Blushing: He was accused of plagiarizing his first serious poetry submission.

The Rest of the Story: As a high school student, twentieth century American poet John Ashbery hoped to have his poems published in a local journal. However, when he mailed in a piece, he received a simple reply of "Sorry." The rejection wasn't because Ashbery lacked talent—the editors thought he had plagiarized the poem. One of Ashbery's classmates had been so impressed with his work that he had already submitted the same poem, thinking Ashbery would be too humble to do it himself.

★ ★ ★ ★ ★

LIAR, LIAR DIPLOMA ON FIRE

The Culprit: L. Ron Hubbard

Why He's Blushing: He got caught lying on his résumé.

The Rest of the Story: For years psychological-thriller writer L. Ron Hubbard bragged about his prestigious education. He said he graduated from George Washington University as a nuclear physicist, but school records show that he dropped out after two years—

during which he failed physics and was on probation for poor grades. He also claimed to have received a Ph.D from California's Sequoia University. It was exposed as a mail-order diploma.

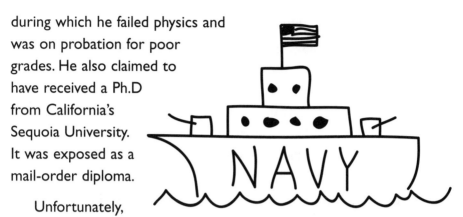

Unfortunately, academics wasn't the only area of life that Hubbard felt the need to embellish. While in the Navy, Hubbard claimed his crew detected Japanese submarines approaching California and spent seventy-two hours bombing (depth charges) the area and celebrating that they had sunk at least one of the enemy ships. However, later investigations revealed that there were never any foreign subs— Hubbard had simply been firing at a "magnetic deposit" in the ocean.

★ ★ ★ ★ ★

MULTIPLE PERSONALITY "DISORDER"

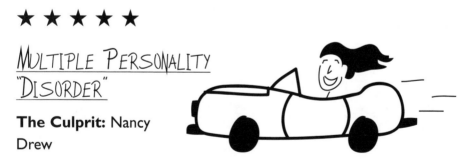

The Culprit: Nancy Drew

Why She's Blushing: The authors who wrote about her couldn't keep their stories straight.

The Rest of the Story: One of the most popular mystery series of the twentieth century, *Nancy Drew* featured a strong protagonist.

However, among the multiple authors who wrote under the pen name Carolyn Keene, Nancy's story just couldn't stay straight. Some of the books briefly mention that Nancy's mother died when Nancy was just ten years old—others claim she was three. In some of the books, Nancy's snooping counterpart is named Buck Rodman—others call him Burt Eddleton. Originally a blonde, the sleuth is referred to as "titian-haired" (or strawberry blonde) in later books. She also has an incredible number of cars for such a young girl. Her blue roadster suddenly turns maroon, then green, then black. In later books she instead has a coupe and a blue convertible.

If changes in appearance and sidekicks weren't enough, Nancy also becomes more politically correct as the authors change hands and revised reprints are made of the original stories. For example, the early first edition manuscripts contained a handful of negative stereotypes about Asians and Hispanics. Nancy also used to be sneakier. She carried a revolver, trespassed on private property, and "stole" her evidence. More recent versions describe her as a more passive, law-abiding sleuth.

★ ★ ★ ★ ★

MAVERICK'S BIG MISTAKE

The Culprit: Roald Dahl

Why He's Blushing: He tried to land at an airport that didn't exist.

The Rest of the Story: While serving in the Royal Air Force in the fall of 1940, Dahl received an assignment to fly his Gladiator from Egypt to Libya. The trip was so long that it required multiple stops to refuel. However, while attempting to land for the final time, Dahl fumbled and couldn't see the airstrip below. Running out of fuel quickly, he had to navigate in the dark and make an emergency landing in the middle of the desert. The undercarriage of the plane smacked a boulder as it skidded in the sand, resulting in a horrific crash. Dahl cracked his skull, smashed his nose, and was suddenly blinded. After being rescued, he received word that there was no airstrip in that part of the desert—he had been looking for a plot of land that didn't even exist. His sight finally returned after eight weeks of hospital care.

★ ★ ★ ★ ★

 THE BLUSHING BIOGRAPHY

The Culprit: Christina Rosetti

Why She's Blushing: Her biographer told the world that a dead mouse caused all of her problems.

The Rest of the Story: Born in London in 1830, Christina Rosetti was a beautiful little girl who spoke Italian and won the

When poet Christina Rosetti was a young adult, she shunned the theater because the actors had a lazy "moral tone," quit playing chess because she noticed that she was "too eager to win," and regularly fasted. She even refused to go into the Mummy Room of the British Museum because she feared the world would come to an end and the corpses would come to life before her eyes.

hearts of many. However, she was a little odd when it came to animals. Once, while visiting her grandpa in Buckinghamshire, she came across a dead mouse. Feeling sorry for the vermin, she buried it. A few days later, she returned to see how it was doing. When she dug up the moss, a big beetle scurried out. Rosetti ran away screaming and never went back—but her biographer, Virginia Moore, read a little further into the situation. It may be a stretch, but Moore believes Rosetti was affected by her encounter with the beetle for the rest of her life. In a chapter she wrote in *Distinguished Women Writers* (E.P. Dutton & Co., Inc., 1903), Moore attributes Rosetti's heart trouble, cancer, chronic cough, and "disease of the eyes" to the fear that resulted from the event, a fear her brother referred to as "skeletons in Christina's various closets."

★ ★ ★ ★ ★

THE NUDIE CONTROVERSY

The Culprit: Shirley Jackson

Why She's Blushing: Her college advisor wouldn't let her print photos of naked men in her literary magazine.

The Rest of the Story: While in college at Syracuse

University, short-story guru Shirley Jackson lost her job working for *The Syracusan* humor magazine when the decision was made that it would no longer include fiction. For a new job, she decided to start her own on-campus literary publication, *The Spectre*, named after a line from a William Blake poem. Thanks to campus censorship, however, her first issue didn't come out as intended. With fifty mimeographed pages ready to be bound and distributed, she was stopped by an advisor who told her the unthinkable: she wasn't allowed to print naked photos! In an editorial in the following issue, Jackson explained to her readers:

> Here we are, already a magazine with a lurid past. Just before our first issue was bound … the English department (working through our faculty advisor) tapped us on the shoulder gently and informed us that we were a menace to public morals. It seems we had two pictures of nude male bodies, and if you want to have nude bodies in a campus publication, without corrupting morals, they have to be female bodies.

Needless to say the images came out, but after the rag's distribution other people spoke up and wrote letters of complaint that there was plenty more "dirty" content in the form of stories that would make anyone blush in mixed company.

Chapter 6

And Then They Were Young: Cheesy Childhood Anecdotes

And Then They Were Young: Cheesy Childhood Anecdotes

Whether they were seriously spoiled, touted as geniuses or punished for bending the rules at school, these creative youngsters give a whole new meaning to the term "kidding around."

DID YOU KNOW

Tennessee Williams birth name was Tom Williams, but he changed it. His ancestors were "Indian-fighting Tennesseans," and his friends gave him the nickname because of his soft Southern drawl.

LIVIN' IN THE SPOOK HOUSE

The Call of the Wild author **Jack London was desperate for attention as a boy.** With a mother too busy planning séances and get-rich-quick schemes, he was stuck being toted around by his stepsister, Eliza. At just four years old, he would join nine-year-old Eliza at school because he had nowhere else to go. He would flip through picture books while the other children practiced writing in cursive. At

In the late 1800s, Jack London worked making burlap in a jute mill for $1 per day and at an electrical company shoveling coal.

home, he often got wrapped up in his mother's wacky experiments. He claims that when he was six, his mother set him on a table during a séance, and the table levitated off of the floor. London's friends called his home "the spook house" and were afraid of his mother's whooping and hollering when she claimed to be "possessed" by a spirit.

CHICKEN RUN BACKWARDS

One of Savannah, Georgia's claims to fame is being the hometown of acclaimed author Flannery O'Connor. It wasn't the most exciting place to grow up, however. The most interesting thing that ever happened to her as a child? **She owned a pet chicken**

who walked backwards. Later, she lived on a farm and took care of hundreds of birds, including peacocks, ducks, and hens.

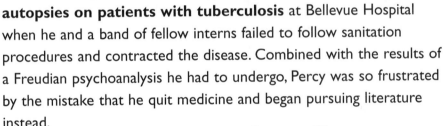

★ ★ ★ ★ ★

TAKE AN ANTIBIOTIC AND CALL ME IN THE MORNING

While in medical school in the early 1940s, Lancelot author **Walker Percy was conducting autopsies on patients with tuberculosis** at Bellevue Hospital when he and a band of fellow interns failed to follow sanitation procedures and contracted the disease. Combined with the results of a Freudian psychoanalysis he had to undergo, Percy was so frustrated by the mistake that he quit medicine and began pursuing literature instead.

★ ★ ★ ★ ★

DUSTY TREASURES

When Southern-born writer Rick Bragg was a young boy, his estranged father gave him two gifts—a 22-caliber rifle and three boxes of old books, including everything from William Shakespeare and Mark Twain to Sir Arthur Conan Doyle and Ernest Hemingway. His father, of course, didn't really know who any of those writers were. He just knew that the books looked pretty with their faded, leather-wrapped covers. They looked like something rich people would own, he said. Bragg's father warned him that if there were any pornographic books in there, he should toss them out before his mother caught sight of them. Luckily, they were all classics.

★ ★ ★ ★ ★

It's All in the Genes

Seeking a "normal" reputation, **Lord Byron spent much of his life desperately trying to live down the rowdy, rakish ways** of his ancestors—especially his grand uncle, the fifth Lord Byron, who was notorious for causing a ruckus. He attempted to kidnap a famous actress, killed his cousin in a duel, and built a miniature castle and fort on a lake for no reason at all. Regardless of Byron's efforts to escape his grand uncle's actions, however, he was often mocked. He was born with a club foot, and for some time his mother couldn't afford to buy him a corrective shoe and brace.

CHEESY MOMENTS OF CONTROVERSY
Lord Byron's nurse, May Gray, was fired for being drunk, violent, and sexually precocious with him before he was even a teenager.

★ ★ ★ ★ ★

THE TEA TIME TROUBLEMAKER

A rebel at heart, J.R.R. Tolkien liked to cause trouble while students at King Edward's School in Birmingham, England, kept their noses in the books. He and three friends formed a secret society they called the Tea Club and Barrovian Society, or T.C.B.S. They would buy tea in Barrow's Stores and sneak it into the school library (which was prohibited). What rebels.

★ ★ ★ ★ ★

AN ENCOUNTER WITH ICKY INSECTS

As a boy, Christian writer **Clives Staples (C.S.) Lewis had an unusual fear of insects**. Its origin? A pop-up children's book. Lewis had once seen a photo of a giant stag beetle towering over a tiny Tom Thumb-like character. Made from cardboard, the bug's horns came off

DID YOU KNOW?

C.S. Lewis' parents often called him by one of his many nicknames—Jack, Jacko, Kricks, and Klicks.

the page at Lewis as if they were going to pinch his little fingers. It was his earliest memory of fear, and from that day on Lewis never overcame his disdain for insects. His mother felt guilty and called the book an "abomination," something she never should have allowed in a nursery.

★ ★ ★ ★ ★

THE GLOATING GENIUS

Call him a savant or not, but Robert Browning was a whiz. At just twelve years old he had written his first book of poetry. Like a true hormone-ridden pre-teen, however, he destroyed it when it was turned down by a handful of publishing companies. A bit of a snob when it came to getting along with the other kids at school, Browning ended up being taught by a private tutor most of his life. By age fourteen, he was fluent in five different languages and by age sixteen he enrolled as a freshman in London's University College. Continuing his childhood disdain for the organized classroom, however, he dropped out after just two semesters.

★ ★ ★ ★ ★

A Tale of Six Shillings

Charles Dickens was a regular at his hometown boot-blacking factory, and while most children his age were playing cops and robbers, he worked ten hours a day gluing labels on jars of shoe polish in a room overrun with rats. His family was stuck in a debtor's prison, and Dickens took his father his earnings, six shillings a week, to support them as they paid off their debts. Once a socialite, Dickens' father had gone broke entertaining the public and desperately trying to maintain his status as a bigwig. The writer never forgave his family for making him work in such harsh, crowded factory conditions—and until his death in 1870, he made the plight of the working class a focus of his literature.

★ ★ ★ ★ ★

Payback's a Snitch

Poet turned-playwright Tennessee Williams never had much interest in masculine things. A lengthy illness during his childhood had made him both passive and sensitive. Williams' father, Cornelius, was embarrassed by his effeminate ways and often teased him about how he needed to be more of a man. He even called him "Miss Nancy" to get on his nerves. But Williams ultimately got his revenge—he wrote his father's personality into many of his scripts. Big Daddy, the overbearing and overly masculine (even abusive) protagonist from *Cat on a Hot Tin Roof*, was one way Williams released his anger over the way his father ridiculed him as a child.

★ ★ ★ ★ ★

THE SPOILED SON

The youngest of six children, *Charlotte's Web's* **E.B. White garnered all the pampering that a little brother can expect**. Being the youngest—and being born just before his father started making big bucks—White was the talk of the town. He was the first child on his block to own a bicycle and bragged about a sixteen-foot green canoe his father got him when he was just eleven. Daddy didn't just give him material things, though. For his twelfth birthday, White's father wrote him a note on Park Avenue Hotel stationery reminding him, "You have been born in the greatest and best land on the face of the globe under the best government known to men. Be thankful then that you are an American."

When E.B. White, born Elwyn Brooks White, was a child, he believed that his birthday—July 11—was a lucky day because the numbers seven and eleven were lucky numbers.

★ ★ ★ ★ ★

PRETENDING TO PREACH

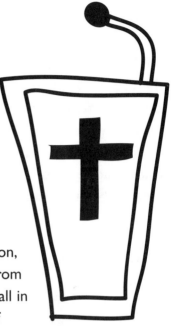

As a boy, Thomas Hardy was quite the do-gooder. On rainy days, he would wrap himself in his mother's tablecloth, stand on a chair, and read the family's morning prayer aloud. His cousin would shout the "Amens," and his grandmother, acting as the mock congregation, would clap while eating breakfast. Hardy would give a short sermon, piecing together things he remembered from the priest's most recent speeches. It was all in good fun, but Hardy was actually afraid of growing up. He didn't like hearing people talk about becoming a man. He liked his jokes and his lazy childhood ways. Despite Hardy's liking to act like a child, it hurt his mother's feelings when he told her of his wish to stay a boy forever.

★ ★ ★ ★ ★

PUPPY LOVE GOES KA-PUT

Like most adolescents, F. Scott Fitzgerald was obsessed with girls during his late teenage years. Despite many college crushes, one in particular stayed with him much of his life. He met Ginevra King on one of the last days before Christmas break in 1915. She was from a wealthy Chicago family, and the two instantly became pen pals, writing their passionate feelings for each other back and forth. By the end of the year, however, Fitzgerald had dropped out of Princeton because of illness and poor grades. He wrote in his diary about being crushed that the romance had fizzled and he subsequently rarely heard from King.

> F. Scott Fitzgerald eventually earned the riches he once admired in his college crush. Although he made plenty of cash off the books he published, he spent thousands keeping up his socialite status.

★ ★ ★ ★ ★

THE [ABBREVIATED] BIRDS AND BEES

Daphne du Maurier came from a family that was extremely shy about sexual matters. When she turned twelve years old, du Maurier's mother gave her a speech about her impending menstrual cycle: "You mustn't be surprised if something not very nice happens to you in a few weeks … it can't be stopped … it goes on happening, every month, until [you] are middle aged, and then it stops." That was all the counseling she received, and she was even forced to swear that she would not blab about the "occasion" to her little sister, Jeanne. Du Maurier dreaded the day, even holding tight to a dream that maybe she would turn into a boy before her first menstruation.

★ ★ ★ ★ ★

DANCING KING

Although his father protested because of the family's devout religious beliefs, **Ernest Hemingway's mother enrolled him and his siblings in dance lessons.** A former opera singer, Grace Hall Hemingway loved the arts and encouraged her children to do so as well. Despite the artsy façade, Hemingway grew up to join his father as an avid sportsman with a love for hunting and fishing.

★ ★ ★ ★ ★

TOSSING OUT THE CARBS

As a boy, playwright Arthur Miller had a part-time job at a New York bakery delivering fresh bread and rolls every morning before he went to school. They expected their bread to be on time. Unfortunately, while riding his bicycle through town one sleepy morning, Miller

hit a patch of ice, and rye bread, onion rolls, and pumpernickel flew in every direction. Panicked, he gathered them up as quickly as he could. Unfortunately, it wasn't long before he realized he could never repack the bags accurately. Instead of returning to the bakery, he decided to make it fair. Every bag got an equal amount of bread—and he ate the leftovers.

★ ★ ★ ★ ★

An Unlikely Critique

When he was barely thirteen years old, Henry Wadsworth Longfellow had one of his very first poems, "The Battle of Lovell's Pond," published in the Portland *Gazette*. When his father picked up the paper the morning it was delivered, Longfellow waited eagerly for a compliment, but no one seemed to notice. Later that evening, he hoped that at least his father's friends had seen his work of genius. They had, but their response wasn't exactly complimentary. Not

> # DID YOU KNOW?
> Henry Wadsworth Longfellow's poems often reflected his strong aversion to war, which may have been influenced by the early death of his uncle, a Navy lieutenant, who was his namesake.

knowing who was the author of the poem, one friend commented that what he had read that morning was "very stiff. It is all borrowed, every word of it." Too embarrassed to tell them the poem had been his, Longfellow kept his mouth shut and cried himself to sleep.

★ ★ ★ ★ ★

POOR BUT PRUDENT

Born the son of a tweny-two-year-old shoemaker in Denmark, **Hans Christian Andersen lived in a one-bedroom shack.** Regardless of his cramped quarters, Andersen's imagination took off at a young age. He memorized entire Shakespeare plays and recited them, using wooden dolls as actors on a toy stage he built.

At one point, Andersen's father believed the family was related to nobility. The Father Hans Christian Andersen Center has records that Andersen's grandmother spilled the beans and told him he was secretly upper-class. However, there is no official historical proof of the

TALES OF THE RUDE AND CRUDE

In his free time, Hans Christian Andersen worked in a cigarette factory with co-workers so crude that they would place bets on whether or not he was actually a girl.

matter. The Andersens did have some connections to Danish royalty, but they were simply part of a business relationship.

★ ★ ★ ★ ★

A TALE OF TWO PERSONALITIES

Joseph Conrad showed signs of a slightly bi-polar personality as a teenager. He flip-flopped between being extremely reserved and organized to impulsive and dangerously wanton. When he was seventeen, his romantic notions of life on the sea led him to a career onboard a boat. In 1874, he joined the Spanish Carlists. After years as a gun runner, he wrecked the ship that his uncle had helped him finance and gambled away the rest of his savings.

★ ★ ★ ★ ★

THE FREUDIAN FAKER

A whiny little daydreamer, Jewish author **Elie Wiesel caused his parents to panic when they noticed he had lost weight** and became suddenly picky about what foods he wanted to eat. They spent hundreds of dollars going from doctor to doctor to ask about his weight loss and his headaches. However, Wiesel had no plans for getting better; he used his complaints as an excuse to skip school even when he was well. It wasn't because he hated school—it was because he was addicted to being around his mother. Wiesel loved staying at home in bed where he could hear her working around the house. When she would leave to help at the family store, he would suddenly feel abandoned and afraid. Even when Wiesel was at school, he counted down the minutes until they would be reunited.

★ ★ ★ ★ ★

A Story of Stump Babies

The author of *The Color Purple: A Novel*, **Alice Walker was always playing jokes on her siblings**—even while in the womb! In fact, when she was born, her older sister had wanted another child around the house so bad that she was fooled by African-American folklore. Based on a Southern myth that babies came from stumps, Ruth had spent several years looking around the yard for a new sister. She even nearly drowned once while peeking into a tree that was next to a creek to see if there was a little baby inside. When her mother went into labor with Alice, Ruth hid in the closet to see how the stump would be brought in. She later realized that Alice had come from her mother's belly.

★ ★ ★ ★ ★

GIRL OF GOTH

Amelia Atwater-Rhodes is well known among modern writers of young-adult fiction. She finished her first vampire novel at just thirteen years old, and even then she had a handful of other incomplete stories sitting at home just waiting to be finished. Amelia's family and friends didn't always believe that she was a natural with a pen, however. While touring a local high school as an eighth grader, one of her friends bragged to a teacher that Amelia had already written a book. He took a look at her work and was so blown away by the maturity in her writing that he became her literary agent. Since then, Amelia has been featured in *The New Yorker, Entertainment Weekly, Seventeen Magazine, USA Today,* and on a variety of national morning shows.

★ ★ ★ ★ ★

DO AS I SAY, NOT AS I DO

In the 1900s, thriller-writer Eric Ambler's parents performed in troupes as the incredible "Reg and Amy Ambrose," but they wouldn't let their eager teenage son join in the fun. They wanted him to do something more respectable with his life—to get as far away from the stage as possible. He got an engineering scholarship to London University, but it wasn't long before he was writing song lyrics and plays.

THE SHOE-IN STORY

When acclaimed fiction writer Josephine Haxton began writing, she would often send early versions of her manuscripts to friends for their edits and opinions. One was so impressed that he showed it to his boss at Houghton Mifflin, and the editor called Haxton personally to tell her that he would like to submit the novel for an upcoming fellowship competition. Haxton was hesitant, afraid that the book would not be complete in time. However, he talked her into it, saying, "If you want me to help you make up your mind … if you will enter the competition, your novel has won."

TEA-TIME TYPING

Herman Melville's heritage always pointed him to the sea. His grandfather, Major Thomas Melville, partied hard during the

Boston Tea Party in 1773. For years, Herman's eyes were glued to a piece of memorabilia on his grandfather's mantel—a bottle of tea that he had squeezed from his wet clothes after the event.

Chapter 7

Fun Facts About Your Favorite Children's Authors

Fun Facts About Your Favorite Children's Authors

They say good writers write what they know, but these children's book authors didn't always enjoy the idyllic lives presented in their stories. In real life, they suffered from writer's block and were afraid of being kidnapped. They were accused of being serial killers and had their books censored. Here's some other wacky stuff you never knew.

S.E. Hinton loves horseback riding and reading, but her true love may be taking classes at local colleges (not for credit). When she has time to sit down and write, Hinton says she first writes on paper in longhand, then types into a computer later.

S.E. HINTON, THE OUTSIDERS

The Outsiders gave novelist S.E. Hinton a quick dose of fame, but with the fanfare came a lot of pressure. Being nicknamed "The Voice of the Youth" was just too much for Hinton, and she quickly became overwhelmed. The pressure resulted in three years of writer's block. Luckily for Hinton, her boyfriend wouldn't put up with the slump and began insisting that she write two pages every day if she wanted to leave the house. The ploy worked, and her career has been strong ever since.

★ ★ ★ ★ ★

PHILIP PULLMAN, DARK MATERIALS

Young-adult author Philip Pullman has found himself in hot water in the past, accused of actively denouncing Christianity. He has, in fact, denounced C.S. Lewis's classic *Chronicles of Narnia* as faith-based propaganda. In response he wrote his own series that remarkably resembled Lewis's. His *Dark Materials* and *The Chronicles of Narnia* both tell the story of talking animals and children entering

144

parallel worlds at odds with each other. Like *The Lion, the Witch and the Wardrobe*, the first book in the *Dark Materials* series features a girl hiding in an old wardrobe. Despite the similarities, there is still a difference—critics have accused Pullman of actively rejecting some of Lewis's themes. For example, Pullman believed Lewis created false hope for children with cancer or children whose parents have cancer when he penned a fictional cure for the disease in one of the Narnia books.

★ ★ ★ ★ ★

Lois Lowry, The Giver

Born in Hawaii, Lowry was originally named "Sena" after her Norwegian grandmother. However, once the grandmother got word of the baby's new name, she quickly sent a telegraph to try and change Lowry's parents' minds. Why shouldn't the girl have an American name? she asked. After a bit of coaxing from grandma, who obviously didn't care about serving as the child's namesake, Lowry's father changed her name to Lois, after one of his sisters.

Lowry's most controversial book, *The Giver*, has received both rave reviews and harsh criticism across the United States. In 2005, the Associated Press reported that a group of disgruntled parents were picketing to remove the book from their children's eighth grade reading list. They argued that it was "sexually explicit" and "violent." Regardless of the group's insistence that nothing should enter a child's mind that is not positive and uplifting, the school board voted to keep the book in school as planned.

★ ★ ★ ★ ★

ALEKSEY NIKOLAYEVICH TOLSTOY, NIKITA'S CHILDHOOD

A writer from Soviet Russia, Tolstoy started out a rich man. In 1900, his father died, leaving him thirty thousand roubles and a family name worth even more. He was proud of his heritage, but he also mocked it while playing dirty tricks on his friends. Tolstoy bought a truckload of random antique portraits and hung them around his fancy home. When he had visitors, he would take them from portrait to portrait, talking about the legacy of the "family members" in each one. When they would leave, however, Tolstoy would laugh with friends about how he had no idea who was in the portraits and had completely fabricated the stories about his family's respectable past.

★ ★ ★ ★ ★

ERIC CARLE, THE VERY HUNGRY CATERPILLAR

Few children know that one of their favorite interactive picture books, *The Very Hungry Caterpillar,* was originally titled *A Week with Willi*

Worm. The star of the original plot? A bookworm. However, Carle's editor was concerned that children wouldn't be huge fans of a big green worm. In the end, the story was translated into more than fifty different languages worldwide. In 2005, a copy of the book was sold every fifty-seven seconds.

FRANCES HODGSON BURNETT, THE SECRET GARDEN

As an adult, Frances Hodgson Burnett was so good at storytelling and pretending that she often found it difficult to get along with fellow grown-ups. Bored around people her own age, Burnett would light up when children begged her to tell them stories. Even when she was

At just seven years old, Frances Hodgson Burnett was obsessed with the fiction she found in magazines such as *Young Ladies' Halfpenny Journal, London Society,* and *Godey's Lady's Book.* Mimicking the tales she was used to reading, Burnett spun her own stories for peers and family. It wasn't long before she was submitting stories to *Godey's* editor Sara Lucretia Hale, who didn't believe such a young girl could have written such good British fiction. She made Burnett write a second story to prove the legitimacy of the first.

at parties with friends, she would find excuses to run off with the kids. She loved to surprise them by playing fairy godmother. On one occasion, she waved her opera glasses about and pulled a toy boat from behind her back—a toy she had known one of the little boys wanted. He was so enthused by the trick that he didn't care about the boat—he asked her for the "wand" instead.

★ ★ ★ ★ ★

BEATRIX POTTER, THE TALE OF PETER RABBIT

The creator of the classic mischievous bunny who sneaks under the fence into Mr. McGregor's garden, Beatrix Potter grew up with parents who lived solely off of their inheritances—neither of them worked. Potter was raised by nannies, and when she was old enough to go to school, they banned her from intellectual development and instead made her a housekeeper. She became so lonely that she often snuck little animals into the home to keep her company—something that is reflected in the stories she wrote as an adult. Potter's parents were so strict that they even refused to approve her engagement to publisher Norman Warne because he worked for a living. They would rather their daughter lead a life of lazy luxury just like them.

★ ★ ★ ★ ★

ROALD DAHL, JAMES AND THE GIANT PEACH

At just eight years old, Roald Dahl was joking around with four of his best friends at school when he came up with a brilliant game—what if they put a dead mouse in a jar of candy at the local sweet shop? Dahl didn't like the owner anyways; he described her as a "mean and loathsome" old woman named Mrs. Pratchett. Like most children concocting sneaky plans against adults, Dahl was caught in the act and was whipped by the headmaster at his school. From then on, Dahl's parents sent him to a long list of boarding schools.

As much as Dahl hated boarding schools, however, it was while he was studying at Repton School that the Cadbury chocolate company began sending boxes of new recipes to be taste-tested by students. For years he dreamed of inventing his own chocolate bar that would wow Mr. Cadbury himself. The experience served as his inspiration for the book *Charlie and the Chocolate Factory*.

> In 1920, when Roald Dahl was only three years old, his older sister died of appendicitis and his father died of pneumonia.

149

★ ★ ★ ★ ★

DAV PILKEY, CAPTAIN UNDERPANTS

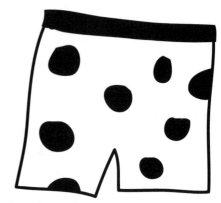

Born in 1966 in Cleveland, Ohio, Dav Pilkey was quite the disruptive student in elementary school. Later diagnosed with Attention Deficit Disorder, he was often forced to move his desk out into the hallway, where he would work on writing the comic book stories he hid in his desk. Pilkey was called David until he worked in a pizza parlor, where his boss accidentally spelled his name "Dav" on a nametag. His friends got a kick out of the mishap, and though he may not have worked in the restaurant business for long (he published his first book at nineteen years old), the nickname stuck.

★ ★ ★ ★ ★

BRIAN JACQUES, TRIBES OF REDWALL SERIES

When Brian Jacques' teacher told him to go home and write a story about animals for homework one day, he came up with a cute little tale about a

Before he became a full-time writer, Brian Jacques worked as a policeman, truck driver, boxer, bus driver, comic, sailor, and folksinger. Today he enjoys reading but says he avoids reading other children's-book authors' work to avoid unintentional plagiarism.

bird whose job was to clean a crocodile's teeth. The story was so impressive that his teacher had him caned by the principal for plagiarism. Regardless, Jacques loved the topic and spent the rest of his life writing about animals. However, some critics believe Jacques endorses social class systems by suggesting that the "good" and "bad" characters in his book are based on particular species. For example, squirrels, hedgehogs, and mice are usually praised, while foxes and rats are portrayed as stupid and greedy.

★ ★ ★ ★ ★

LEWIS CARROLL, ALICE IN WONDERLAND

With a story as bizarre as *Alice in Wonderland*, it's no wonder Lewis Carroll's life is surrounded by wild rumors. In 1996, a fellow author named Richard Wallace published a book called *Jack the Ripper, Light-Hearted Friend* that directly accused Carroll of being one of two men involved in the infamous Jack the Ripper serial killings. However, both Carroll and Thomas Vere Bayne, the other man accused, came up with perfect alibis for the nights of each murder. Carroll had expressed vague interest in the cases, but there was never any substantial evidence connecting him to the crimes.

★ ★ ★ ★ ★

SELMA LAGERLÖF, JERUSALEM

A Swedish children's author, Selma Lagerlöf became a part of the Swedish Academy, a group that nominates people for and awards the Nobel Prize in literature. She was such a generous woman that when World War II began, she sent her own Nobel Prize medal to Finland to help the government finance its battle against the Soviet Union. The group was so honored by the gesture that they couldn't possibly sell it or melt it down, so they said thank you and returned it promptly.

★ ★ ★ ★ ★

ASTRID LINDGREN, PIPPI LONGSTOCKING

When Swedish author Astrid Lindgren began dreaming of her concept for the funky, impulsive Pippi Longstocking, she was greatly inspired by Lucy Maud Montgomery's *Anne of Green Gables*. Like protagonist Anne, Pippi has red hair, freckles, and

As of 1995, Astrid Lindgren's *Pippi Longstocking* books had been translated into fifty-six languages and sold four million copies in Germany alone.

an assertive attitude. The name of Pippi's home, Villa Villekulla, is even a lighthearted reference to the Swedish name of Anne's home—Grönkulla. Unfortunately, when translated to English some of Lindgren's humor is lost. For example, in Swedish "pippi" means crazy.

★ ★ ★ ★ ★

VERNA AARDEMA, WHY MOSQUITOES BUZZ IN PEOPLE'S EARS

This famous author had never considered writing for children until she got frustrated with her own daughter, who refused to eat dinner until she got a bedtime story first. The little girl was brilliant at the bribes, and Verna often came up with tales related to communities and countries she had recently read about.

★ ★ ★ ★ ★

A.A. MILNE, WINNIE-THE-POOH

Few people know that author A.A. Milne was most inspired by his son's collection of stuffed animals, which included a bear named Winnie-the-Pooh. As for the one human character in Milne's popular series, Christopher Robin was named after his son.

★ ★ ★ ★ ★

HANS AUGUSTO REY, CURIOUS GEORGE

While living in Paris one year, Hans was recognized as such a talented artist that a French publisher practically begged him to write a children's book about animals. It wasn't long before *Rafi and the Nine Monkeys* hit the shelves, but they weren't much of a hit. However, one of the book's characters, Curious George, was so loved by children that Hans made him the star of his own story. The writer's new work was interrupted by

the beginning of World War II, when he fled Paris on a bicycle with his wife before the Nazis intervened. One of the few things he chose to take with him—the manuscript for *Curious George*.

★ ★ ★ ★ ★

LOUIS SACHAR, SIDEWAYS STORIES FROM WAYSIDE SCHOOL

Sachar's first book for children, *Sideways Stories From Wayside School*, was accepted for publication during his first week as a law school student. A few years earlier, Sachar had signed up as a volunteer at a local elementary school. He was asked to be the Noon Time Supervisor, who keeps an eye on the children while they eat lunch. Instead of being an authority figure, however, Sachar played games with them, earning him the nickname "Louis the Yard Teacher." Memories of those times stuck with him the all through law school, and after he passed the bar exam he decided to be a full-time writer.

★ ★ ★ ★ ★

BEVERLY CLEARY, RAMONA QUIMBY SERIES

At four years old, Cleary's first experience with a book was a frightening one. Living on an Oregon farm, she was invited by a neighbor to borrow a picture book any time she wished. However, the woman's son loved to tease Cleary, convincing her that he had sold her for a nickel to another neighbor, Quong Hop, who would soon be moving back to China. Falling for the joke,

Cleary had to walk past the Hop home every time she wanted to borrow the book. She would slither through the grass like a snake so no one would see her and snatch her off to Asia.

E.B. WHITE, CHARLOTTE'S WEB

When his publisher first accepted the manuscript for *Charlotte's Web* in 1952, **E.B. White could only receive payments up to $7,500 a year in royalties**, allowing him to collect money from the book's success over a longer period of time. Twenty-seven years later, when he decided it was time to liquidate all assets due him, he collected a lump sum of more than half a million dollars. Needless to say, a large chunk of that check went to taxes.

Beverly Cleary has never tried out her book manuscripts on children because they are "conditioned to please adults" and never answer honestly.

While in school, E.B. White developed a paralyzing fear of public speaking and has declined every invitation to speak in public since then.

★ ★ ★ ★ ★

MICHAEL BOND, PADDINGTON BEAR

When Michael Bond first wrote the Paddington Bear series, **many people assumed Paddington was drawn after a bear native to Peru,** the spectacled bear. However, no one has ever proven a resemblance between the bear in the books and the photos from the wild.

Chapter 8

Cocktail Party Conversation: Useless Trivia

Cocktail Party Conversation: Useless Trivia

Do you know **Pippi Longstocking's full name? What author gave his birth date to a friend? Who really wrote the Little House** books? **What did many historic authors use as "inspiration" for writing? Use these juicy tidbits about your favorite authors to spice up your next cocktail party and stump your friends.**

- Author Robert May wrote "Rudolph, the Red-nosed Reindeer" in 1939. While brainstorming the story, he initially considered naming the famed reindeer Rollo or Reginald.

- At the age of fourteen, Anna Sewell fell while walking home from school in the rain, injuring both her ankles. The injury was likely not treated correctly, and she became lame for the rest of her life, unable

to stand or walk for any length of time. For greater mobility, she frequently used horse-drawn carriages, which contributed to her love of horses and concern for the humane treatment of animals. As she wrote *Black Beauty*, she dictated the text to her mother or wrote on slips of paper that her mother later compiled.

- Ralph Ellison's favorite books as a child were *Wuthering Heights*, *The Last of the Mohicans,* and *Jude the Obscure*.

- "Tintern Abbey" was one of the only poems William Wordsworth ever wrote that he didn't completely change through revisions and editing.

- *Pride and Prejudice* author Jane Austen was so humble and shy about her writing that no one ever caught her with a pen in hand. "No matter how suddenly one arrives, she has heard the door close … and hidden the white sheets," writes biographer Virginia Moore.

- *Pride and Prejudice* was originally titled *First Impressions*.

- Pippi Longstocking's full name is Pippilotta Provisionia Gaberdina Dandeliona Ephraimsdaughter Longstocking.

- When *Treasure Island* author Robert Louis Stevenson died in 1894, he put in his will that his November 13 birthday be gifted to a friend who hated her Christmas birthday.

- Born around 635 BC, Sappho was considered one of the first poets—she is remembered as "The Poetess"—while Homer, who was one of the only other poets to precede her, is remembered as "The Poet." Sappho's poems were first written on waxed wooden blocks before papyrus was discovered. Her works have survived through being quoted in Greek, Roman, and Egyptian documents. Only one of her poems exists in completion—"Hymn to Aphrodite"—which was quoted by Dionysius of Halicarnassus in 25 BC.

- When she was forty years old, Emily Dickinson said of Shakespeare's writings, "Why is any other book needed?"

- Critics of the Little House books often question just how involved Laura Ingalls Wilder's daughter, Rose, was in penning the series. Some argue that she was simply an encourager who helped her mother get in touch

with publishers and agents. However, others believe that Rose took the rough drafts and transformed them into the magical stories they are known as today.

- When short-story writer Eudora Welty was twenty-six years old, she offered her first story, "The Death of a Traveling Salesman," to be published in a little magazine that could not pay her for it. Until that point, she had never studied writing in college, nor had she ever belonged to a literary group.

- Washington Irving wrote *Rip van Winkle* overnight while staying with his sister in Birmingham, England.

- Some historic authors may have gotten their "inspiration" from fungi that feed on old papers. A British medical journal once reported that they can be hallucinogenic and can cause "enhancement of enlightenment" in readers.

- John Grisham is a distant cousin of former president Bill Clinton.

- Irish writer John Banville's wife described him as "a murderer who's just come back from a particularly bloody killing" when he sat down to write.

- Most famous for writing the play *Rozencrantz and Guildenstern Are Dead* and the screenplay for *Shakespeare in Love*, Tom Stoppard also edited scripts for *Indiana Jones and the Last Crusade* (1989), *Sleepy Hollow* (1999), and *The Widowmaker* (2002).

- Like most widowers, poet Sylvia Plath's husband took over her personal and literary estates when she committed suicide in 1963. He had overseen the publication of many of her manuscripts for years, but to protect her privacy he destroyed the journal encompassing three years of their relationship.

- Considered the father of the African novel, Chinua Achebe has received more than thirty honorary degrees from universities around Canada, South Africa, Scotland, England, Nigeria, and the United States. The schools include Dartmouth, Harvard, Brown, Cape Town, and Southampton.

- The original stage version of *The Wonderful Wizard of Oz* was quite different from L. Frank Baum's book. In fact, it was aimed at adults instead of children. Toto was replaced by a new character named Imogene the Cow, and included a waitress and a streetcar operator, among Dorothy's gang of fellow victims. On stage, Baum even had actors make critical references to Theodore Roosevelt, Senator Mark Hanna, and oil tycoon John D. Rockefeller.

- Isaac Asimov once said, "If my doctor told me I had only six minutes to live, I wouldn't brood. I'd type a little faster."

- At least twenty-one publishers rejected Golding's *Lord of the Flies* before Faber and Faber printed it in 1954.

- Rudyard Kipling died of a brain hemorrhage in 1936. He was seventy years old. However, it wasn't the first time his death was publicly announced. Several years earlier it was incorrectly printed as fact in a magazine. When he read the statement, he wrote, "I've just read that I am dead. Don't forget to delete me from your list of subscribers."

- While helping develop the James Bond films in 1962, writer Ian Fleming asked directors to let his cousin, actor Christopher Lee, play villain Dr. Julius No.

- Some believe that naturally left-handed *Alice's Adventures in Wonderland* author Lewis Carroll suffered psychologically by being forced to use his right hand.

- A treasure map with an X marking the location of the buried treasure is one of the most familiar pirate props, yet it is entirely a fictional invention which owes its origin to *Treasure Island* author Robert Louis Stevenson's original map.

- As a college student, poet Paul Blackburn became pen pals with the famed Ezra Pound. He even hitchhiked to Washington, D.C., a few times to pay his friend a visit in the hospital.

- Once when *Inferno* author Dante Alighieri was walking down the street in Verona—where his work was well known—he overheard a couple of women gossiping about him. One of the women, obviously commenting loudly enough for the author to overhear, crossed herself, then said, "Do you not see how his beard is crisped and his colour darkened by the heat and some down there?" She was referring to hell, of course.

- When poet Bob Kaufman heard about the assassination of John F. Kennedy, he was inspired by Buddhism to take a vow of silence. He didn't speak again until the end of the Vietnam War in 1975. His first words after several long years? He recited the poem "All Those Ships that Never Sailed."

- To please his father, William Golding enrolled in Oxford's Brasnose College as a science major before finally switching to his true love—English and poetry—after his junior year.

- Best known for his Church of Scientology self-help books, L. Ron Hubbard is an Eagle Scout.

- British science-fiction writer John Wyndham's real name is John Wyndham Parkes Lucas Beynon Harris.

- Belgian writer Georges Joseph Christian Simenon was able to write sixty to eighty pages a day and published 450 novels and short stories during his career.

- Children's author Gary Paulsen was a regular competitor at the Iditarod. He had to give up sledding and sold his dogs in 1990 because of heart problems. However, after more  than a decade in retirement sailing throughout the Pacific Ocean, he returned to the sport in 2003. He was supposed to compete in the 2005 Iditarod tournament but withdrew shortly before the race began.

- When Birmingham, Alabama, native and nationally acclaimed poet Sonia Sanchez was born in September 1934, her parents couldn't agree on a name for their second daughter and instead let relatives decide. They chose Wilsonia Benita. Her mother died during childbirth, and Wilsonia spent the next nine years going from relative to relative.

- Geoffrey Chaucer's father was kidnapped in 1324 by one of his aunts, who hoped he would force his son to marry her daughter. She was arrested and fined £250.

- Ralph Ellison's father, who died in a car accident when Ralph was just three years old, named his son after Ralph Waldo Emerson and had dreams that he would one day be a poet.

- Romance-novelist-turned-mystery-writer Janet Evanovich admits on her web site that at one point in her career, she collected rejection letters sent to her by publishers. When the box started overflowing, she would "burn the whole damn thing," put on some pantyhose, and head out to find some temp work.

- In 1932, *Death of a Salesman* author Arthur Miller couldn't afford to go to college so he worked as a truck driver, a waiter, and in an auto-parts warehouse for $15 per week.

- When poet Audre Geraldine was born, she didn't cry. She was so nearsighted that doctors thought she was legally blind. She didn't start talking until she learned how to read at four years old. It was at this point that she changed the spelling of her name, Audrey, because she did not like how the "y" hung down below the other letters. She opted to leave the "y" off, and she has spelled it that way ever since.

- In high school, Audre Geraldine became literary editor of the school arts magazine and had her first love poem published in *Seventeen*.

- The poet Lord Tennyson loved "tavern food" including stead, cheese, and new potatoes.

WHERE WE GOT THIS STUFF

Abraham, Gerald. *Tolstoy*. New York: Haskell House Publishers, 1974.

Allen, William Rodney. *Walker Percy: A Southern Wayfarer*. Jackson: University Press of Mississippi, 1986.

Ambrosetti, Ronald J. *Eric Ambler*. New York: Twayne Publishers, 1994.

Angelou, Maya. *Hallelujah! The Welcome Table*. New York: Random House, 2004.

——. *All God's Children Need Traveling Shoes*. New York: Random House, 1997.

Auslander, Joseph and Frank Ernest Hill. *The Winged Horse: The Story of the Poets and their Poetry*. New York: Doubleday, Doran & Company, 1930.

Barker, Juliet. *A Life: Wordsworth*. New York: Harper Collins, 2000.

Barry, Elaine. *Robert Frost*. New York: Continuum Publishing, 1988.

Bauder, David. "Benchley Wouldn't Write Same 'Jaws' Today." *The Trentonian*, April 5, 2000.

Bixler, Phyllis. *Frances Hodgson Burnett*. Boston: Twayne Publishers, 1984.

Bragg, Rick. *All Over But The Shoutin'*. New York: Vintage Books, 1997.

Busby, Mark. *Ralph Ellison*. Boston: Twayne Publishers, 1991.

Cady, Edwin H. *Stephen Crane*. Boston: Twayne Publishers, 1980.

Calhoun, Richard J. and Robert W. Hill. *James Dickey*. Boston: Twayne Publishers, 1983.

Carpenter, Humphrey. *JRR Tolkien: A Biography*. Boston: Houghton Mifflin Company, 2000.

——. *W.H. Auden: A Biography*. Boston: Houghton Mifflin Company, 1981.

Clarke, Gerald. *Capote: A Biography*. New York: Avalon Publishing Group, 1988.

Clinton, Paul. "Along Came a Spider spins tangled, dull tale." April 6, 2001. http://archives.cnn.com/2001/SHOWBIZ/Movies/04/06/review.spider/index.html

Dowden, Edward. *Robert Browning*. London: J.M. Dent & Co., 1904.

Eble, Kenneth. *F. Scott Fitzgerald*. Boston: Twayne Publishers, 1963.

Elledge, Scott. *E.B. White: A Biography*. New York: W.W. North & Company, 1984.

Evans, I.O. *Jules Verne and his work*. Boston: Twayne Publishers, 1966.

Fensch, Thomas, ed. *Coversations with John Steinbeck*. Jackson: University Press of Mississippi, 1988.

French, Warren. *J.D. Salinger*. Boston: Twayne Publishers, 1963.

Friedman, Lawrence S. *Wiliam Golding*. New York: The Continuum Publishing Company, 1993.

Friedman, Lenemaja. *Shirley Jackson*. Boston, Twayne Publishers, 1975.

Garson, Helen S. *Tom Clancy: A Critical Companion*. Connecticut: Greenwood Press, 1996.

Gillespie, Stephenie Miller. "Police Confirm Disappearance of Local Boy, Age 10." *The Midland Star*, December 15, 2004.

Hardy, Florence Emily. *The Life of Thomas Hardy*. Connecticut: Archon Books, 1970.

Hayman, Ronald. *Arthur Miller*. New York: Frederick Ungar Publishing, 1972.

Hays, Peter L. *Ernest Hemingway*. New York: Continuum Publishing, 1992.

Hewlett, Dorothy. *Elizabeth Barrett Browning: A Life*. New York: Alfred A. Knopf, 1952.

Higginson, Thomas Wentworth. *Henry Wadsworth Longfellow*. Boston & New York: Houghton Mifflin Company, 1902.

Hillway, Tyrus. *Herman Melville*. Boston: Twayne Publishers, 1979.

Inge, Tonette Bond. *Southern Women Writers: The New Generation*. Tuscaloosa: The University of Alabama Press, 1990.

Jacobs, Eric. *Kinglsey Amis: A Biography*. New York: St. Martin's Press, 1995.

Jeppson, Janet, ed. *Isaac Asimov: It's Been a Good Life*. New York: Prometheus Books, 2002.

Kaplan, Justin. *Walt Whitman: A Life*. New York: Simon and Schuster, 1980.

Kelly, Richard. *Daphne du Maurier*. Boston: Twayne Publishers, 1987.

Kermode, Frank. *John Donne*. London: Longmans, Green & Co Ltd., 1957.

Lauber, John. *The Inventions of Mark Twain: A Biography*. New York: Hill and Wang, 1990.

Levi, Peter. *Tennyson*. New York: Charles Scribner's Sons, 1993.

Kronick, Joseph G. "Vachel Lindsay's Life." *Modern American Poetry*. http://www.english.uiuc.edu/maps/poets/g_l/lindsay/lindsay_life.htm

Kulii, Beverly Threatt and Ann E. Reuman and Ann Trapasso. "Audre Lorde's Life and Career." *Modern American Poetry*. http://www.english.uiuc.edu/maps/poets/g_l/lorde/life.htm

MacDonald, Ruth K. *Dr. Seuss*. Boston: Twayne Publishers, 1988.

McIntyre, Ian. *Robert Burns: A Life*. New York: Welcome Rain Publishers, 2001.

Metcalf, Eva-Maria. *Astrid Lindgren*. New York: Twayne Publishers, 1995.

Meyers, Jeffrey. *Robert Frost: A Biography*. London: Constable and Company, 1996.

——. *Katherine Mansfield: A Biography*. New York: New Directions Books, 1978.

Middlebrook, Diane Wood. *Anne Sexton: A Biography*. Boston: Houghton Mifflin Company, 1991.

Moore, Virginia. *Distinguished Women Writers*. New York: E.P. Dutton & Co., Inc, 1903.

Morgan, Janet. *Agatha Christie*. New York: Alfred A. Knopf, 1985.

Murray, Brian. *Charles Dickens*. Continuum Publishing: New York, 1994.

Nelson, Benjamin. *Arthur Miller: Portrait of a Playwright.* New York: David McKay Company, 1970.

Parker, Jamie. "Who Is Buried in Edgar Poe's Grave?" United States Naval Academy Website. http://www.usna.edu/EnglishDept/poeperplex/gravep.htm

Pearson, Hesketh. *Sir Walter Scott: His Life and Personality.* New York: Harper & Brothers Publishers, 1954.

Pflieger, Pat. *Beverly Cleary.* Boston: Twayne Publishers, 1991.

Porter, Katherine Anne. "A Curtain of Green." *Eudora Welty.* Chelsea House Publishers: New York, 1986.

Roberts, Bette B. *Anne Rice.* New York: Twayne Publishers, 1994.

Rosenburg, Bruce A. *Ian Fleming.* Boston: Twayne Publishers, 1989.

Ryley Robert M. "Kenneth Fearing's Life." *Modern American Poetry.* http://www.english.uiuc.edu/maps/poets/a_f/fearing/life.htm

Sinclair, Andrew. *Jack: A Biography of Jack London.* New York: Pocket Books, 1977.

Tischler, Nancy M. *Tennessee Williams.* Austin: Steck-Vaughn Company, 1969.

Trueblood, Paul G. *Lord Byron.* Boston: Twayne Publishers, 1977.

Tucker, Martin. *Joseph Conrad.* New York: Frederick Ungar Publishing, 1976.

Warnke, Frank J. *John Donne.* Boston: Twayne Publishers, 1987.

White, Evelyn C. *Alice Walker: A Life.* New York: W.W. Norton & Company, 2004.

Wiesel, Elie. *All Rivers Run to the Sea: Memoirs.* New York: Schocken Books, 1995.

Wilson, A.N. *C.S. Lewis: A Biography.* New York: WW Norton & Company, 1990.

Zeiger, Henry A. *Ian Fleming: The Spy Who Came In with the Gold.* New York: Duell, Sloan and Pearce, 1965.

WE ALSO USED THESE SOURCES:

www.evanovich.com

www.wikipedia.org

The Thomas Hardy Association, www.yale.edu/hardysoc

African American Literature Book Club, http://aalbc.com/authors/maya.htm

www.litencyc.com/php/speople.php?rec=true&UID=5876

James Thurber's Comic Vision, www.todayinliterature.com/stories

The Edgar Allan Poe Society of Baltimore, www.eapoe.org

www.fyodordostoevsky.com

www.woodyallenband.com

www.stephenking.com

www.online-literature.com/dumas

www.cnn.com

www.online-literature.com/kipling/
www.nationalgeographic.com/grimm/article.html
www.randomhouse.com/kvpa/eastonellis
www.peterbenchley.com.
www.uselessknowledge.com
www.ianwatson.info/news.html
www.ltolstoy.com
www.online-literature.com/gertrude-atherton
www.sehinton.com

ABOUT THE AUTHOR

Camille Smith Platt is a freelance writer and the Editor of *Chattanooga Christian Family* magazine. A graduate of the Samford University Department of Journalism and Mass Communication, she has also done research and writing for national trivia magazine *mental_floss* and Birmingham lifestyle magazine *PORTICO*. Her love-hate relationship with trivia stems from a fascination of quirky knowledge and a lifetime of always being stumped. She and her husband, Daniel, live in Chattanooga, Tennessee.

YOU MAY ALSO ENJOY THESE OTHER BOOKS IN THE REAL CHEESY SERIES.

Real Cheesy Facts About: U.S. Presidents

ISBN-13: 978-1-57587-248-3

ISBN-10: 1-57587-248-X

Real Cheesy Facts About: Rock 'n' Roll

ISBN-13: 978-1-57587-251-3

ISBN-10: 1-57587-251-X

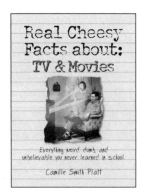

Real Cheesy Facts About: TV & Movies

ISBN-13: 978-1-57587-249-0

ISBN-10: 1-57587-249-8